CONNECTIONS AND SEPARATIONS

Divorce, Name Change and Other
Genealogical Tidbits
from the ACTS
of the
VIRGINIA GENERAL ASSEMBLY

WESLEY E. PIPPENGER

HERITAGE BOOKS
2007

HERITAGE BOOKS

AN IMPRINT OF HERITAGE BOOKS, INC.

Books, CDs, and more—Worldwide

For our listing of thousands of titles see our website
at
www.HeritageBooks.com

Published 2007 by
HERITAGE BOOKS, INC.
Publishing Division
65 East Main Street
Westminster, Maryland 21157-5026

International Standard Book Number: 978-1-58549-578-8

INTRODUCTION

During the 18th and 19th centuries, countless petitions were presented to the Virginia General Assembly by individuals or groups. These were primarily requests that laws be made or changed, facilities or services be established, for grants of restitution for losses, or relief from difficulties or unfortunate situations. The list of actual subjects is extensive, and the records best describe these.

Several compilers collected and published the decisions of the General Assembly, for the period 1619 to about 1806. Of these, the most well known are William Waller Hening and Samuel Shepherd. Beginning in 1807 the Virginia government arranged to have the Acts published at the end of each full session. These can be found in book form or on microfilm at the Library of Virginia in Richmond and other major research institutions.

This work is a selection of transcripts gleaned from the published Acts of the Virginia General Assembly. The purpose in presenting these is to demonstrate the wealth of valuable information that they contain—information that is frequently overlooked by researchers.

The focus of the present collection is divorces and name changes. Every instance of these two activities that was found in the published acts has been included here. Information that is linked to at least 105 Virginia counties includes 155 divorces and 44 name changes for the period 1789 to 1853. A sampling of some of the more interesting items found while collecting the divorces and name changes has been included in the hope that they will entice readers to search the Acts themselves.

While the text of these abstracts provides useful information, the researcher should also use them as the beginning of a trail which leads to county records, possible court cases and depositions from family and friends. Following these trails can often provide additional information on the reason for a legislative petition and add to the researcher's information on the family, neighbors and their interrelations.

Items are presented in chronological order, as they appear in the original published records. Also included here are a few legislative petitions for which a published Act was not found. These are presented to demonstrate the many cases where a petition was unsuccessful or otherwise did not progress all the way through the chain to result in a published Act. A full comparison of the surviving original legislative petitions (which are among the collections at the Library of Virginia) to the published Acts has not been done by this compiler. Such a project of great magnitude has been left to be done at another time.

Wesley E. Pippenger
Arlington, Virginia
April 2000

CONNECTIONS AND SEPARATIONS:
Divorce, Name Change and Other Genealogical Tidbits
from the Acts of the
Virginia General Assembly

1789. Chapter LXXIX. – An ACT concerning the marriage of Ann Dantignac

(Passed the 19th of December, 1789)

WHEREAS a marriage was solemnized in the month of September, in the year of our Lord one thousand seven hundred and eighty, between John Dantignac then of Colchester, in the county of Fairfax, and Ann Peachy of the county of Prince William; And whereas it has been represented to the Assembly, that soon after the marriage took effect, he began, and so long as they lived together continued to treat his wife in a cruel and inhuman manner; That in the month of July in the year one thousand seven hundred and eighty-three, he departed from this state with a declared resolution never to return to it, or to see his wife again, whereby he has abandoned her to the world, and as far as he might has relinquished the character and duties of a husband; That he has not since discovered any disposition to resume his former connexion with the said Anne, but has lived with another woman in adultery; *Be it therefore enacted*, that it shall and may be lawful for the said Anne to sue out of the office of the general court, a writ against the said John Dantignac, which writ shall be framed by the clerk, shall express the nature of the case, and shall be published for eight weeks successively in some one of the public papers, whereupon the plaintiff may file her declaration in the said cause, and the defendant may appear and plead to issue in which case, or if he does not appear within two months after such publication, it shall be set for trial by the clerk on some day in the succeeding court, but may for good cause shewn to the court be continued until the succeeding term.

Sect. 2. Commissions to take depositions and subpaenas to summon witnesses shall issue as in other cases.

Sect. 3. Notice of taking depositions published in some one of the public papers shall be sufficient.

Sect. 4. A jury shall be summoned, who shall be sworn well and truly to enquire into the allegations contained in the declaration or to try the issue joined as the case may be, and shall find a verdict according to the usual mode; and if the jury in case of issue joined, shall find for the plaintiff, or in case of enquiry into the truth of the allegations contained in the declaration, shall find in substance that the defendant hath abused and deserted the plaintiff, and that he hath lived in adultery with another woman, the said verdict shall be recorded, and thereupon the marriage between the said John and Anne shall be totally dissolved; the power of the said John over the person and property of the said Anne shall intirely cease: and the said Anne is hereby declared to be from and after recording te said verdict to every intent and purpose a *feme sole*.

1794. Chapter LVI. – An ACT for suspending the proceedings on a certain forthcoming Bond, entered into by Ciceley Anderson, Administratrix of William Anderson, deceased.

(Passed the 14th of December, 1794)

BE it enacted by the General Assembly, That all further proceedings on a bond entered into by Ciceley Anderson, as administratrix of William Anderson, deceased, by virtue of an act of Assembly, passed in the year one thousand seven hundred and ninety-two, intituled, "An act for suspending certain executions," for the forthcoming of certain property belonging to the estate of her late husband, taken to discharge the arrears of taxes due from him as sheriff of the county of Hanover, for the years one thousand seven hundred and eighty nine, and one thousand seven hundred and ninety, shall be, and are hereby suspended for the term of one year from the passing of this act.

Sec. II. THIS act shall commence and be in force from and after the passing thereof.

1794. Chapter LVII. – An ACT concerning Sarah Tool and Dorothy Tanner.

(Passed the 18th of December, 1794)

BE it enacted by the General Assembly, That Sarah Tool, widow of Richard Tool, (who during the late war enlisted as a gunner on board of the *Henry Galley* belonging to this commonwealth, and died in the services thereof) shall be placed on the list of pensioners, and allowed the sum of eight pounds per year.

Sec. II. *AND be it further enacted*, That Dorothy Tanner, the widow of Jacob Tanner, a soldier, who was in the service of this state during the late war, and died in the same, shall be placed on the list of pensioners, and allowed the sum of eight pounds a year.

Sec. III. *AND be it further enacted*, That the auditor of public accounts shall, and he is hereby authorised and required, on application to him made, to issue to the said Sarah Tool and Dorothy Tanner, a warrant on the treasurer for the sum of twelve pounds each for their immediate relief.

Sec. IV. THIS act shall commence and be in force from and after the passing thereof.

1794. Chapter LXIII. – An ACT vesting in the Heirs of William Pittman, deceased,
a certain Tract of Land therein mentioned.

(Passed the 12th of December, 1794)

BE it enacted by the General Assembly, That all the right, title, and interest which the commonwealth hath in or to a certain tract of land lying in the county of King George, which hath escheated to the said commonwealth, as the property of a certain William Pittman, who was condemned and executed for the crime of murder, shall be, and the same is hereby vested in John Pittman, Ann Pittman, Mary Pittman, and William Pittman, children and heirs of the said William Pittman, deceased, to be by them held and enjoyed in the same manner as if it had legally descended to them.

Sec. II. SAVING however to all and every person or persons, body politic and corporate, other than the commonwealth, any right, title, or interest which ne or they

2

might or would have had to or to the said land, or any part thereof if this act had never been made.

Sec. III. THIS act shall commence and be in force from and after the passing thereof.

1794. Chapter LXIV. – An ACT vesting in the Widow and Heirs of James Dixon, deceased, a tract of Land whereof John Richmond, died seized.
(Passed the 12ᵗʰ of December, 1794)

B E *it enacted by the General Assembly*, That all the right, title, and interest which the commonwealth hath, or may have in or to a certain tract of land lying in the county of Louisa, which hath escheated to the said commonwealth, as the property of a certain John Richmond, who died seized thereof, intestate and without lawful heirs, shall be, and the same is hereby vested in Lucy Dixon, widow and relict of James Dixon, deceased, who was the natural and reputed son of the aforesaid John Richmond, deceased, and in Sarah, John, Nancy, and Patsey, children and heirs of the said James, to be by them held and enjoyed in the same manner as if it had legally descended to them.

Sec. II. SAVING however to all and every person or persons, body politic or corporate (other than the commonwealth) any right, title, or interest which he or they might or would have had in or to the said land or any part thereof if this act had never been made.

Sec. III. THIS act shall commence and be in force from and after the passing thereof.

1796. Chapter LXXV. – An ACT for paying to the administrator and administratrix of Thomas Elder, deceased, the money produced by sale of his lands, for the purposes therein mentioned.
(Passed December the 12ᵗʰ, 1796)

W HEREAS it is represented that Thomas Elder, late of Henrico county, died, leaving sundry debts unpaid, and seized of certain lands which, remaining undevised by his will, escheated to the commonwealth, and have been sold according to law:

BE it enacted by the General Assembly, That the treasurer be, and is hereby required and directed, after deducting from the proceeds of the sale or sales of the said lands, which have been or may be paid into the treasury, all lawful costs and charges, allowed or paid on account of such sale or sales, to pay to John Potts, and Anna Evans, administrator and administratrix, with the will annexed of the said Thomas Elder, deceased, the balance remaining of the said proceeds, which shall be by them in a due course of administration applied to the payment of the debts of the said Thomas Elder, deceased, and after such application, should there then remain a surplus of the proceeds aforesaid, that the same may be retained by the said Anna Evans, as a retribution for certain personal property devised to her by the said Thomas Elder, which has been sold for the payment of his debts.

3

1796. Chapter LXXVII. – An ACT authorising Peter Caverley to lease, for the benefit of the Orphans of David Arell, certain Lots whereof he died seized, in the town of Alexandria.

(Passed December the 10th, 1796)

WHEREAS it is represented, that a certain David Arell, late of the town of Alexandria, departed this life, leaving two infant children by the names of Richard and Christiana, and seized of several lots of land in the said town, which by his will he directed to be granted by his brother Samuel Arell, for the benefit of such children; that the said Samuel Arell hath since died, without complying fully with the directions aforesaid:

BE it enacted by the General Assembly, That Peter Caverley, who hath been duly appointed guardian of the said children, be, and is hereby authorised and empowered, during their minority, to grant in fee, or for a shorter time, if he shall think proper, all and every such lot or lots, agreeably to the directions of the will of the said David Arell, as were not granted by the said Samuel Arell at the time of his death; reserving the best rent he can obtain for the same, to the said Richard and Christiana, and their heirs respectively, according to the will of the said David Arell.

1798. Chapter XCII. – An ACT for placing Robert Leonard on the List of Pensioners.

(Passed January the 6th, 1798)

BE *it enacted by the General Assembly*, That Robert Leonard, who served as a soldier in the late war, and is unable to obtain a subsistence by labor, shall be placed on the list of pensioners, and be allowed the sum of forty dollars annually.

Sec. II. THE Auditor of public accounts on application to him, made either in person or by attorney, shall issue to the said Robert Leonard, a warrant for the sum of forty dollars for his immediate relief, to be discharged in like manner as other pension warrants.

Sec. III. THIS act shall commence and be in force from and after the passing thereof.

1798. Chapter XCIII. – An ACT for placing William Brabstone on the List of Pensioners.

(Passed January the 5th, 1798)

BE *it enacted by the General Assembly*, That William Brabstone, who entered into the late war as a soldier, in the year one thousand seven hundred and seventy-six, and continued therein until the end thereof, and from a wound received in his shoulder at the battle of Brandy-Wine, together with the fatigue and hardships which he suffered in the army, is unable to obtain a subsistence by labour, shall be placed on the list of pensioners and be allowed the sum of forty dollars annually.

Sec. II. THE Auditor of public accounts, on application to him made, either in person or by attorney, shall issue to the said William Brabstone, a warrant for the sum of forty dollars for his immediate relief, to be discharged in like manner as other pension warrants.

Sec. III. THIS act shall commence and be in force from and after the passing thereof.

1798. Chapter LXXXIX. – An ACT for allowing a Sum of Money to Elizabeth Mann.
(Passed January the 6th, 1798)

B E it enacted by the General Assembly, That there shall be allowed and paid to Elizabeth Mann, widow of Thomas Mann, who was killed by Indians in one thousand seven hundred and ninety four, while in the service of his country, the sum of forty-dollars annually for four years, for her relief.

Sec. II. THIS act shall commence and be in force from and after the passing thereof.

1798. Chapter XCIV. – An ACT for placing several Persons on the Pension List, and for other Purposes.
(Passed the January 22d, 1798)

B E it enacted by the General Assembly, That Charles Clements, of the county of Fluvanna, who in consequence of several wounds received as a soldier in the service of his country during the late war, is rendered unable to support himself, shall be, and he is hereby placed on the list of pensioners, and shall receive an allowance of forty dollars annually.

Sec. II. BE it further enacted, That John Shepperd of the county of Kanawha, who from a wound received in an expedition against the Indians in one hand and thigh, is rendered unable to support himself, shall be placed on the list of pensioners, and shall be allowed and paid the sum of forty dollars annually.

Sec. III. AND be it further enacted, That Elizabeth Jameson, widow of Alexander Jameson, late of the county of Prince George, deceased, shall be allowed and paid by the Treasurer, upon warrant from the Auditor of public accounts, annually, during her life, the sum of two hundred dollars, to be paid at the same time, and in like manner as other pensions are paid; and for the immediate relief of the said Elizabeth Jameson, the Auditor of public accounts shall be, and he is hereby authorised and required, to issue to the said Elizabeth Jameson, a warrant or warrants on the Treasurer, for two hundred dollars.

Sec. IV. THIS act shall commence and be in force from and after the passing thereof.

1799. Chapter LXVII. – An ACT concerning George Willis.
(Passed January 2, 1799)

B E it enacted by the General Assembly, That the auditor of public accounts shall be, and he is hereby authorised and required to issue to George Willis, who, by reason of wounds received while in military service, in the course of the late war, has been rendered unable to support himself by labor, a warrant or warrants for the sum of sixty dollars, for his immediate relief, be discharged by the treasurer out of any money in the treasury not otherwise appropriated by law.

Sec. II. This act shall commence, and be in force, from and after the passing thereof.

1799. Chapter LXVIII. – An ACT concerning the Heirs of Peter Francis de Tubeuf, deceased.
(Passed January 2, 1799)

BE it enacted by the General Assembly, That Francis and Alexander de Tubeuf, surviving heirs of Peter Francis de Tubeuf, deceased, be and they are hereby allowed until the first day of January, one thousand eight hundred and four, to repay the balance which may be due of a sum of money advanced by the commonwealth, on a loan to the said Peter Francis de Tubeuf, in his lifetime, to enable him and certain French emigrants, who came with him into this commonwealth, to settle their lands in the county of Russell.

Sec. II. This act shall commence and be in force from and after the passing thereof.

1799. Chapter LX. – An ACT to discontinue the Pension heretofore allowed to Benjamin Blackburne.
(Passed January 23, 1799)

WHEREAS it appears to the General Assembly, that Benjamin Blackburne, now an inhabitant of the state of Tennessee, draws an annual pension of fifty dollars from the treasury of this commonwealth, and is not an object who ought to come within the benefit of the pension law:

Sec. I. Be it therefore enacted, That from and after the passing of this act, the said pension shall be discontinued.

Sec. II. All acts coming within the purview of this act are hereby repealed.

1799. Chapter LXXXI. – An ACT for the immediate relief of Charles M'Graw.
(Passed January 25, 1799)

BE it enacted, That Charles M'Graw, who was a soldier in the Virginia line during the late war, and was disabled at West Point, in the year one thousand seven hundred and seventy-eight, while in performance of his duty, which disability has now so far increased as to render him totally unable to support himself by labour, be allowed the sum of sixty dollars; and that the auditor of public accounts issue to the mayor of the city of Richmond, as trustee, for the said Charles M'Graw, a warrant on the treasurer for the said sum, as an immediate relief and support, until application can be made to the general government on behalf of this unfortunate man.

1799. Chapter LXXXII. – An ACT vesting in James Swinton and Anna Swinton, certain Lands therein mentioned.
(Passed January 3, 1799)

BE it enacted by the General Assembly, That all the right, title and interest, which the commonwealth hath or may have, in or to a certain tract of land lying in the county of Caroline, whereof George Swinton died seized, and which, by his last will

6

and testament, he devised to his nephew, James Swinton, who was then an alien, and which land, in consequence thereof, escheated to the commonwealth, shall be, and the same is hereby vested in the said James Swinton, who is now a citizen of the said commonwealth, to be by him held and enjoyed in the same manner as if he had been born a citizen of the said commonwealth.

Sec. II. *And be if further enacted*, That all the right, title and interest, which the commonwealth hath, or may have, in or to one other tract of land whereof the said George Swinton also died seized, containing about seven hundred and ten acres, lying in the said county, and which was purchased by the said George Swinton of James Robb and Joseph Richerson, subsequent to the date of his said will, shall be, and the same is hereby vested in Anna Swinton, widow and relict of the said George, and in the said James Swinton, to be held by them as tenants in common: Provided, however, that the buildings on the said land shall be, and are hereby allotted to the said Anna, without any account or valuation thereof; saving, however, to all and every person or persons, bodies politic and corporate, (other than the commonwealth) any right, title or interest, which he or they might, or would have had, in or to the said tracts of land, or any part thereof, if this act had never been made.

Sec. III. This act shall commence, and be in force, from and after the passing thereof.

1799. Chapter LXXXIII. – An ACT vesting in the Children of George Gilmer, deceased, certain Lands therein mentioned.

(Passed January 12, 1799)

BE it enacted by the General Assembly, That all the right, title and interest, which the commonwealth hath or may have in or to the following lands, lying in the county of Henry, which George Harmer, by his last will and testament devised to a certain George Gilmer, and which since the death of the said George Gilmer, it is supposed to have become escheatable to the commonwealth, to wit: One tract called *Marrow Bone*, containing by estimation two thousand five hundred and eighty-five acres: one other tract called *Horse Pasture*, containing by estimation two thousand five hundred acres: and one other tract called the *Poison Field*, containing by estimation six hundred sixty seven and an half acres: shall be and the same are hereby released to, and vested in the children, whether heirs or devisees, of the said George Gilmer, deceased, to be by them held and enjoyed according to their respective rights of inheritance or devise under his will (as the case may be) in the same manner as if the said George Gilmer, had died seized of the said lands in fee simple, and an office had been actually found thereof. Saving however to a certain John Lambert, who as heir at law of the said George Harmer, claims the said lands, and to all and every other person or persons, bodies politic and corporate, (other than the commonwealth) any right, title or interest, which he or they might or would have had, in or to the said lands, or any part thereof, against the said children and devisees, if this act had never been made.

Sec. II. This act shall commence in force from the passing thereof.

1803. Chapter LXIV. – An ACT dissolving a marriage between Dabney Pettus and his wife Elizabeth.

(Passed January 4, 1803)

WHEREAS it is represented, That in the month of March, one thousand eight hundred and one, a marriage was solemnized between Dabney Pettus and a certain Elizabeth Morris, who was descended from honest and respectable parents, and was at the time supposed to be unsullied in her reputation; that in the space of four or five months after the said marriage, the said Elizabeth was delivered of a mulatto child, and has since publicly and frequently acknowledged, that the father of the said child was a negro slave, and has voluntarily consented to a dissolution of the said marriage; and the said Dabney Pettus having petitioned the legislature to be divorced from his aforesaid wife; BE *it enacted*, That the said Dabney Pettus shall be and is hereby divorced from the said Elizabeth, and the marriage between said Dabney and Elizabeth, totally dissolved; that the said child be considered as illegitimate & incapable of inheriting any part of the estate of the said Dabney; that the power of the said Dabney over the person and property of the said Elizabeth, shall entirely cease; and she is hereby declared to be a feme sole, and the said Dabney no longer bound by any promise or contract hereafter made or entered into by her.

Sec. 2. *And be it further enacted*, That whatsoever property of the said Elizabeth, the said Dabney had received in consequence of the said marriage, or the value thereof, shall be restored by him to her, or her representatives.

Sec. 3. This act shall be in force from the passing thereof.

1803. Chapter 5. – An ACT giving an annual pension to Rebecca Fulton.

(Passed December 21, 1803)

BE *it enacted by the General Assembly*, That the auditor of public accounts shall, and is hereby commanded to issue a warrant on the public treasury for fifty dollars, to be paid annually to Rebecca Fulton, in consequence of her husband having lost his life in performing his duty, acting under a warrant from a magistrate, in apprehending one Martin, charged with a criminal offence.

2. This act shall commence and be in force from and after the passing thereof.

1803. Chapter 6. – An ACT dissolving a marriage between Benjamin Butt, jun., and Lydia his wife.

(Passed December 20, 1803)

WHEREAS it is represented that in the year one thousand eight hundred and two, a marriage was solemnized between Benjamin Butt, junior, and a certain Lydia Bright, who is of a respectable family, and was at the time of the said marriage supposed to be unsullied in her reputation; that not long thereafter, the said Lydia was delivered of a mulatto child, and has since publicly acknowledged that the father of the said child was a slave, and has voluntarily consented to a perpetual separation between herself and the said Benjamin, who hath petitioned the legislature that he may be divorced from his said wife:

1. *Be it therefore enacted*, That the said Benjamin Butt, junior, shall be and is hereby divorced from the said Lydia, and the marriage between the said Benjamin

8

and Lydia totally dissolved; that the power of the said Benjamin over the person and property of the said Lydia shall entirely cease, and she is hereby declared to be a *feme sole*, and the said Benjamin no longer liable to be bound by any promise or contract which may be made or entered into by her.

    2. *And be it further enacted*, That whatsoever property of the said Lydia the said Benjamin has received in consequence of the said marriage, or the value thereof, shall be restored by him to her or her representatives.

    3. This act shall commence and be in force from and after the passing thereof.

1804. Chapter CVII. – An ACT concerning the heirs of Robert Irwin, deceased.
(Passed February 1, 1804)

B E *it enacted by the General Assembly*, That John Irwin, junior, James Irwin, and Elizabeth Henderson, formerly Elizabeth Irwin, heirs of Robert Irwin deceased, shall be and they are hereby declared to be entitled to the money arising from the sale of the real and personal estate of the said Robert Irwin, which escheated to the commonwealth, by his death, after the payment of the just debts of the said decedent; and that the creditors of the said Robert may have an opportunity of ascertaining their claims.

    Sec. 2. *Be it further enacted*, that they shall be, and are hereby allowed until the first day of January 1805, to prosecute and establish in a legal manner their respective demands, against the estate of the said Robert Irwin, deceased.

    Sec. 3. And the auditor of public accounts is hereby authorised and required, after the expiration of the time aforesaid, to issue to the heirs of the said Robert Irwin deceased, or their attorney, a warrant or warrant for so much money as may remain from the proceeds of the sale of the said escheated property, on the fund arising from escheated property.

    Sec. 4. This act shall commence and be in force from and after the passing thereof.

1805. Chapter XLIII. – An ACT Divorcing Robert Campbell from his Wife Ann.
(Passed January 4th, 1805)

B E *it enacted by the General Assembly*, That a marriage solemnized in the year one thousand seven hundred and ninety four, between Robert Campbell and a certain Ann Alison, shall be, and is hereby dissolved, and the said Robert Campbell forever divorced from the said Ann; that the power of the said Robert over the person and property of the said Ann, shall entirely cease; and that the said Robert shall no longer be bound by any promise or contract which may hereafter be made or entered into by the said Ann.

    Sec. 2. This act shall be in force from the passing thereof.

1805. Chapter XLIV. – An ACT Releasing to Frederick Gauder the Right of the Commonwealth, to a certain Lot of Land.
(Passed January 2d, 1805)

BE it enacted by the General Assembly, That all the right, title and interest, which the commonwealth now hath, or may have, in or to a certain half acre lot of land lying in the Town of Charlottesville, and known therein by the number fifty, and which was purchased by Frederick Gauder of a certain Thomas West, who is since dead, shall be, and the same is hereby released to the said Frederick Gauder, his heirs and assigns.

Sec. 2. Saving to all persons, bodies politic and corporate, except the commonwealth, all rights in or to the aforesaid lot, or any part thereof, in the same manner as if this act had not have been made.

Sec. 3. This act shall be in force from the passing thereof.

1806. Chapter XXXVI. – An ACT Divorcing Ayres Latham from his wife Tabitha.
(Passed January 6th, 1806)

BE it enacted by the General Assembly, That a marriage solemnized between Ayres Latham[1] and a certain Tabitha Latham, shall be, and is hereby dissolved, and the said Ayres Latham forever divorced from the said Tabitha; that the power of the said Ayres over the person and property of the said Tabitha shall entirely cease; and that the said Ayres shall no longer be bound by any promise or contract which may hereafter be made or entered into by the said Tabitha.

Sec. 2. This act shall be in force from the passing thereof.

1806. Chapter LXXXVII. – An ACT to relinquish to Elizabeth Smith, Wife of William Smith, the right of the Commonwealth to certain Tracts of Land.
(Passed February 3d, 1806)

WHEREAS, Charles Neal, late of the county of Montgomery, and commonwealth of Virginia, hath died intestate and without heirs: And whereas, certain lands, of which the said Charles Neal died seized, have become escheatable to the commonwealth; and it appearing to this General Assembly, that Elizabeth, the widow of the said Neal, hath since intermarried with William Smith of the said county:

Section 1. Be it therefore enacted, That all the right, title and interest, of this commonwealth, in all the lands of which the said Neal died seized, or to which he may have had, at the time of his decease, an equitable right, are hereby forever relinquished to the above named Elizabeth. Provided always, That in this act shall be so construed, as in anywise to affect private right.

Sec. 2. This act shall commence and be in force from and after the passing thereof.

---

[1] Published Act gives "Tatham" as the surname; however, the legislative petition which was dated December 13, 1805, Accomack Co., #A38, provides surname "Latham." Also, the petition shows the basis for an absolute divorce by Ayres Latham from his wife Tabitha Latham was that she bore a mulatto child. Reasonable.

1806. Chapter LIX. – An ACT Divorcing Daniel Rose from his Wife Henrietta.
(Passed December 31st, 1806)

WHEREAS it is represented, that in the month of February, in the year one thousand eight hundred and six, a marriage was solemnized between Daniel Rose of Prince-William county,[2] and a certain Henrietta White, who was at that time supposed to be virtuous, and a woman of good character; that in less than seven months thereafter, the said Henrietta was delivered of a mulatto child; that there are reasons to believe that since her said intermarriage, she has permitted a negro slave, the supposed father of the said child, to have a carnal intercourse with her; and that the said Daniel Rose, at the time of his said intermarriage, was, and always since has been, considered as a man of good character; and the said Daniel having petitioned the legislature to be divorced from his said wife:

Section 1. BE it enacted, That the said Daniel Rose shall be, and hereby is, divorced from the said Henrietta, and the marriage aforesaid totally dissolved; that the said child be considered as illegitimate, and incapable of inheriting any part of the estate of the said Daniel; that the power of the said Daniel, over the person and property of the said Henrietta, shall entirely cease; and she is hereby declared to be a feme sole, and the said Daniel no longer bound by any promise or contract hereafter to be made or entered into by her.

Sec. 2. This act shall be in force from the passing thereof.

1806. Chapter 63. – An ACT concerning William Breeden.
(Passed December 31, 1806)

BE it enacted by the General Assembly, That the penalty of one hundred dollars, which was imposed by the county court of King William on William Breeden, for retailing goods, wares and merchandize, without a license obtained from the commissioner of the said county, shall be, to all intents and purposes, fully remitted; and the auditor of public accounts is hereby authorized and required to issue a warrant or warrants to the said William Breeden for one hundred dollars, the amount of the penalty aforesaid, on the public treasury, to be paid out of any monies therein.

2. This act shall be in force from the passing thereof.

1808. Chapter LIX. – An ACT Divorcing Charles Bosher from his Wife Susanna.
(Passed January 9, 1808)

BE it enacted by the General Assembly, That a marriage solemnized between Charles Bosher, and a certain Susanna Wingoe, shall be, and hereby is dissolved, and the said Charles Bosher, forever divorced from the said Susanna; that the power of the said Charles, over the person and property of the said Susanna, shall entirely cease, and that the said Charles, shall no longer be bound by any promise or contract, which may hereafter be made or entered into, by the said Susanna.

2. This act shall be in force from the passing thereof.

---

[2] Legislative Petition, Prince William Co., December 9, 1806, #A5021, Alexander Bruce claims on October 21, 1806, he was present September 5, last past, when Henrietta was delivered of a mulatto child. Numerous signatures. *Reasonable.*

11

1808. Chapter LXX. – An ACT releasing to James Semple and Joanna his wife, the right of the Commonwealth to certain Lands therein mentioned.
(Passed January 20, 1808)

BE it enacted by the General Assembly, That all the right, title, or interest, which the commonwealth hath or may have, in or to the land and lots lying in, and adjoining to that part of the town of Petersburg called *Blandford*, supposed to contain about seventy-two acres, whereof David Black, son of doctor David Black, late of *Blandford* aforesaid, died seized, shall be and is hereby vested in James Semple and Joanna his wife, the said Joanna, being the nearest of kin in the United States, to the said David Black the younger, at the time of his death; to be by the said James Semple and Joanna his wife, held and enjoyed in like manner, as if the same had been purchased by her, in fee.

Saving to all persons, bodies politic and corporate, other than the commonwealth, any right, title, or interest, which they might or would have had, in or to the said land or lots, or any part thereof, if this act had not have been made.

2. This act shall be in force from the passing thereof.

1808. Chapter 62. – An ACT granting to George Douglass and Judy Douglass the duplicate of a certificate.
(Passed January 13, 1808)

BE it enacted by the General Assembly, That the auditor of public accounts is hereby authorized and required to issue to George Douglass and Judy Douglass, a duplicate of a certificate for ninety-one dollars and fifty-six cents, with interest from the twenty-fifth day of June, one thousand eight hundred and two, which was originally issued in the name of Margaret Douglass, on their giving bond and security to indemnify the commonwealth against any damage that may accrue from the issuing such duplicate.

2. This act shall commence and be in force from and after the passing thereof.

1808. Chapter XVII. – An ACT authorising William Waller Hening to Publish an Edition of certain Laws of this Commonwealth, and for other purposes.
(Passed February 5, 1808)

WHEREAS it hath been represented to the present general assembly, by William Waller Hening, that he hath at very considerable trouble and expense, made a collection of all the laws of Virginia now extant, which have been enacted since the first settlement of this country: And whereas the titles to property to a large amount of money of many of the citizens of this commonwealth depend, in many instances, on an act of the general assembly, which exists only in manuscripts, and of which, there is but a single copy; for the preservation of which titles, it is deemed highly expedient, that such of the laws of Virginia, as were passed prior to the year one thousand seven hundred and ninety-two, when the last revisal was made, should be printed and distributed: And the said William Waller Hening, having petitioned the legislature to aid him in the publication of the said laws, and so to provide that they may be considered as of legal authority:

1. *Be it therefore enacted*, That upon the certificate of Creed Taylor, William Wirt, and William Munford, or any two of them, being published with the said laws,

stating that they had carefully compared the edition of the acts so to be published, with the original laws, and found them to be truly and accurately printed, they shall be received and considered of equal authority in the courts of this commonwealth, as the originals, from which they are taken.

2. *And be it further enacted*, That the governor be, and he is hereby authorised and required to subscribe on behalf of the commonwealth, and on such terms, as individuals are permitted to subscribe, for one hundred and fifty copies of the edition proposed to be published as aforesaid, the price whereof shall be paid out of the treasury, upon a warrant or warrants to be issued by order of the executive: *Provided*, That the price shall not exceed five dollars per volume, of six hundred pages large octavo, nor shall more than one volume of the said edition to the number of copies taken by the state be paid for out of the treasury in any one year.

3. *And be it further enacted*, That the copies so subscribed for, on behalf of the commonwealth, shall be distributed by the executive, according to their discretion.

4. This act shall commence and be in force, from the passing thereof.

1808. Chapter XLIII. – An ACT divorcing Margaret Brough from her husband Thomas Brough.
(Passed December 31, 1808)

B E *it enacted by the General Assembly*, That a marriage solemnised between Thomas Brough and Margaret Robertson, shall be, and is hereby dissolved, and the said Margaret forever divorced from the said Thomas; that the power of the said Thomas over the person and property of the said Margaret shall entirely cease, and that the said Thomas shall longer be bound by any promise or contract, which may hereafter be made or entered into by the said Margaret.

2. This act shall be in force from the passing thereof.

1808. Chapter XLII. – An ACT divorcing Nancy Bayne from her husband Griffin Bayne.
(Passed December 31, 1808)

B E *it enacted by the General Assembly*, That a marriage solemnised between Griffin Bayne and Nancy Turner,[3] shall be and is hereby dissolved, and the said Nancy forever divorced from the said Griffin; that the power of the said Griffin over the person and property of the said Nancy, shall entirely cease; and that the said Griffin shall not be bound by any promise or contract which may hereafter be made or entered into by the said Nancy.

2. This act shall be in force from the passing thereof.

---

[3] Legislative Petition, Bedford Co., #A1730, petitioner Nancy J. Bayne, claims that immediately upon marriage, Bayne charged her with unchaste conduct and has made every effort to ruin her reputation and to inflict all possible injuries. *Reported.*

1809. Chapter XLIX. – An ACT divorcing Elizabeth Kimberlin from her husband Martin Kimberlin.
(Passed January 3, 1809)

B E *it enacted by the General Assembly*, That a marriage solemnized between Elizabeth Sponsler and Martin Kimberlin, shall be and is hereby dissolved, and the said Elizabeth forever divorced from the said Martin; that the power of the said Martin over the person and property of the said Elizabeth, shall entirely cease, and that the said Martin shall no longer be bound by any promise or contract, which may hereafter be made or entered into by the said Elizabeth.

2. This act shall be in force from the passing thereof.

1809. Chapter L. – An ACT releasing James Nimmo from the payment of a judgment therein mentioned.
(Passed January 4, 1809)

B E *it enacted by the General Assembly*, That James Nimmo shall be and is hereby released and forever discharged from the amount of a judgment recovered on behalf of the commonwealth against him as surviving executor of William Wishart, deceased, in the general court, on a writ of *scire facias* sued out therein in the year one thousand seven hundred and ninety-nine, reviving a judgment obtained against the said William Wishart in his lifetime, in the year one thousand seven hundred and eighty-three.

2. This act shall be in force from the passing thereof.

1809. Chapter LX. – An ACT Dissolving a Marriage solemnized between West Alricks and Ann Peyton.
(Passed January 9, 1809)

B E *it enacted by the General Assembly*, That a marriage solemnised between Ann Peyton and West Alricks, shall be, and is hereby dissolved, and the said Ann forever divorced from the said West; that the power of the said West over the person and property of the said Ann shall entirely cease, and that the said West shall not be bound by any promise or contract which may hereafter be made or entered into by the said Ann.

2. This act shall be in force from the passing thereof.

1809. Chapter XC. – An ACT concerning certain Certificates and Warrants found among the Papers of John Pendleton, deceased.
(Passed February 3, 1809)

B E *it enacted by the General Assembly*, That the Auditor of public accounts be, and he is hereby authorised and required, to receive into his possession the following certificates and warrants found among the papers of John Pendleton, deceased, viz. One issued the eighteenth day of June, one thousand seven hundred and eighty two, in favor of Joseph Hones, James Terebee and William Burgess, for seven hundred and twenty-one pounds, fourteen shillings and a penny half penny, in full of their demand against John Goodrich, the elder; one issued to captain John Harris, the seventeenth day of December, one thousand seven hundred and eighty

14

two, for seven hundred and fifty pounds, for his brigantine, sails and anchors, which were taken and sold by the committee of safety; one issued the twenty-sixth day of October, one thousand seven hundred and eighty-six, to David Duncan, for three hundred and sixty pounds, for a bill of exchange drawn by George Watt, on the Illinois department; and one issued to William Shannon, the twenty-seventh day of October, one thousand seven hundred and ninety three, for four hundred and thirty-nine pounds, eight shillings and five pence, in part of his claim as quarter-master general to the Illinois regiment; and to issue in lieu thereof, new certificates, bearing interest from the date of this act, for the amount of the original certificates and warrants, which said new certificates, shall issue in the name or names of the owners of the original certificates, and belong to those entitled to the said original certificates.

2. This act shall be in force from the passing thereof.

1809. Chapter XCI. – An ACT divorcing Isaac Fouch from his wife Elizabeth.
(Passed February 4, 1809)

BE it enacted by the General Assembly, That a marriage solemnized between Isaac Fouch and Elizabeth Beach, shall be, and is hereby dissolved, and the said Isaac forever divorced from the said Elizabeth; that the power of the said Isaac over the person and property of the said Elizabeth shall entirely cease, and that the said Isaac shall not be bound by any promise or contract which may hereafter be made or entered into by the said Elizabeth.

2. This act shall be in force from the passing thereof.

1809. Chapter XCII. – An ACT concerning James Scott.
(Passed February 4, 1809)

WHEREAS James Scott, sheriff of Monongalia county, on the eight day of November, one thousand seven hundred and ninety-nine, did by virtue of an execution issued in behalf of the commonwealth against Robert Ferrell for the balance of the revenue tax due for the year one thousand seven hundred and ninety seven, sell a tract of land the property of the said Robert [Ferrell], to Alexander and Robert Hawthorn, for the sum of five hundred and eighty dollars and thirty-three cents, the amount of the said execution and costs, which sum was afterwards by the said James Scott, on the third day of December, one thousand seven hundred and ninety-nine, paid into the public treasury. And, whereas, the said Alexander and Robert Hawthorn, have since been evicted of the said land so sold and conveyed to them by the said James Scott, by the decision of the district court holden at Morgan town, and the said James Scott compelled to repay to them the amount of the purchase money and interest:

1. Be it therefore enacted by the General Assembly, That the auditor of public accounts is hereby authorized and required, to issue a warrant on the public treasury, to be paid out of any money therein, to James Scott, his heirs or assigns, for the sum of five hundred and eighty dollars and thirty three cents, with interest thereon from the third day of December, one thousand seven hundred and ninety-nine, that being the time he paid the amount of the said execution into the public treasury.

2. This act shall commence and be in force from and after the passing thereof.

15

1810. Chapter LVIII. – An ACT concerning Patience and her Children.
(Passed January 16, 1810)

WHEREAS it has been represented to this present General Assembly, That a certain free man of colour by the name of Frank, hath lately departed this life, within the commonwealth, leaving in bondage a widow, named Patience, and three children, Philemon, Elizabeth and Henry, whom the said Frank by his meritorious industry, purchased in his lifetime, but failed to emancipate, and asking the aid of the legislature in obtaining their freedom:

1. *Be it enacted by the General Assembly*, That the aforesaid Patience, widow of the said Frank and the aforesaid Philemon, Elizabeth and Henry his children, henceforth shall be entitled to all the rights and privileges of freedom, as much so as if they had never been in slavery: *Provided always*, That this act shall not be construed to affect the claim of any person or persons whatsoever, against the estate of which the said Frank died seized and possessed.

2. This act shall commence and be in force from the passing thereof.

1810. Chapter LXXI. – An ACT divorcing Abner W. Clopton from his Wife Sally.
(Passed January 23, 1810)

BE *it enacted by the General Assembly*, That a marriage solemnized between Abner W. Clopton and a certain Sally B. Warwick, shall and is hereby dissolved, and the said Abner forever divorced from the said Sally; that the power of the said Abner, over the person and property of the said Sally shall entirely cease, and that the said Abner shall not be bound by any promise or contract which may be hereafter made or entered into by the said Sally.

2. This act shall be in force from the passing thereof.

1810. Chapter CXIII. – An ACT divorcing Leonard Owen from his wife Nancy.
(Passed February 8, 1810)

BE *it enacted by the General Assembly*, That a marriage solemnized between Leonard Owen and a certain Nancy Hampton, shall be, and is hereby dissolved, and the said Leonard forever divorced from the said Nancy; that the power of the said Leonard over the person and property of the said Nancy shall entirely cease, and that the said Leonard shall not be bound by any promise or contract which may hereafter be made or entered into by the said Nancy.

2. This act shall be in force from the passing thereof.

1811. Chapter LXXX. – An ACT concerning Hannah, the daughter of Samuel George, an old Soldier.
(Passed February 11, 1811)

BE *it enacted by the General Assembly*, That it shall be lawful for Hannah, a free woman of colour, who was liberated by the will of William Turner, to whom she belonged in the month of November, in the year one thousand eight hundred and nine, and who is the daughter of Samuel George, also a free man of colour, who served as a marine during the revolutionary war, and she is hereby permitted, to remain as a free person within this state, and to have and enjoy therein all the rights and privileges which other free persons of colour possess and enjoy.

    2. This act shall be in force from the passing thereof.

1812. Chapter CXXXV. – An ACT concerning Betty Dean and others.
(Passed January 6, 1812)

BE it enacted by the General Assembly, That Betty Dean, Frankey Dean, John Dean, Billy Dean, Henry Dean, Daphney Dean, Samuel Floyd, Frank Floyd and Mitchel Floyd, who have lately been emancipated by Margaret Rose and John N. Rose, shall be, and they are hereby permitted to remain in this commonwealth.

    2. This act shall commence and be in force from the passing thereof.

1812. Chapter XCVII. – An ACT releasing to Michael, John, Robert and Thomas Cortney, the right of the commonwealth, to certain lands therein mentioned.
(Passed January 6, 1812)

BE it enacted by the General Assembly, That all the right, title or interest, which the commonwealth hath or may have in or to the following tracts of land lying in the county of Monongalia, to wit; one hundred acres purchased by a certain Michael Cortney, and conveyed to him by deed from Grafton White; twenty-five acres granted to the said Michael Cortney by patent from the commonwealth; and one hundred and eighteen acres, which was also purchased by the said Michael, and conveyed to him by deed from Samuel Hanway; two hundred and fifty acres purchased by a certain John Cortney, and conveyed to him by deed from Benjamin Reeder; and one hundred and eighteen acres which was also purchased by the said John Cortney and conveyed to him by the said Hanway; sixty seven acres and sixteen poles, purchased by a certain Robert Cortney, and conveyed to him by James Tucker; seventy acres, being part of a larger tract of 250 acres, purchased by a certain Thomas Cortney, in his life time, and conveyed to him by deed from said Reeder; (and which seventy acres were, by the last will and testament of the said Thomas Cortney, devised to the said Robert Cortney;) and one hundred and thirty-six and one quarter acres, devised to Thomas Cortney by the last will and testament of his father Thomas Cortney deceased, being part of a larger tract, purchased by the said Thomas Cortney deceased, in his life time, and conveyed to him by the said Benjamin Reeder; all of which is supposed to be escheatable to the commonwealth, shall be and the same are hereby released to the several persons who are in possession of the said lands by conveyance or otherwise as aforesaid; saving, however, to all persons, bodies politic or corporate other than the commonwealth, any right, title or interest, which they might or would have had in or to the said lands, or any part thereof, if this act had not been made.

    2. This act shall be in force from the passing thereof.

1812. Chapter CXXXIV. – An ACT concerning Eve, the wife of Robin Justice, and their children Bowman and Peggy.
(Passed January 18, 1812)

BE *it enacted by the General Assembly*, That when Robin Justice (a free black man of the county of Accomack) shall have regularly emancipated his wife Eve, and their two children, Bowman and Peggy, the said Eve, Bowman and Peggy, shall be, and they are hereby permitted to remain and enjoy the benefit of their freedom in this commonwealth, and shall be entitled to all the rights and privileges which other free persons of colour possess within the same; any law to the contrary notwithstanding.

2. This act shall be in force from the passing thereof.

1812. Chapter XXXII. – An ACT concerning Forfeitures in cases of Suicide.
(Passed February 20, 1812)

BE *it enacted by the General Assembly*, That no forfeiture whatever shall accrue to the commonwealth, in consequence of any suicide. And the estate, whether real or personal, of every person, who shall hereafter destroy his or her own life, or who may heretofore, have destroyed his or her own life, shall pass to the heirs, devisees, legatees or distributees of such person, in the same manner, as if he or she had died from any other cause: *Provided*, that nothing herein contained shall be so construed as to affect any estate whatever, on which an office may have been already found, in favour of the commonwealth.

2. This act shall be in force from the passing thereof.

1812. Chapter CXXXIV. – An ACT concerning Archibald Stuart jun. and Nancy Stuart.
(Passed December 29th, 1812)

WHEREAS it is represented to the General Assembly, by Archibald Stuart junior and Nancy Stuart, infants under the age of twenty one years, in the year one thousand eight hundred and nine, two slaves belonging to them, to wit. Charles a boy and Cynthia a girl, were carried, with the said Archibald and Nancy, from this state to the Illinois territory, by their father, where he intended permanently to reside; but that he has been constrained to return to this state, bringing with him the said Archibald and Nancy, as also their said slaves; –

1. *Be it therefore enacted*, That the said Archibald Stuart jun. and Nancy Stuart shall have full power and authority to retain the said slaves Charles and Cynthia, as their property, within this state, in the same manner as if they had never been carried therefrom: And all penalties and forfeitures, incurred by the bringing the said slaves back to this state, shall be and the same are hereby remitted.

2. This act shall be in force from the passing thereof.

1813. Chapter CII. – An ACT divorcing John Cook from his wife Elizabeth.
(Passed January 1st, 1813)

1. BE *it enacted by the General Assembly*, That a marriage solemnized between John Cook and a certain Elizabeth Been, shall be, and the same is hereby

dissolved, and the said John forever divorced from the said Elizabeth; and that the power of the said John over the person and property of the said Elizabeth shall henceforth entirely cease.

2. This act shall be in force from the passing thereof.

1813. Chapter CXXXV. – An ACT concerning William Gaines.
(Passed January 9th, 1813)

BE it enacted by the General Assembly, That it shall be lawful for the auditor of public accounts, and he is hereby required, to issue, in favour of William Gaines, a warrant on the treasury, for the sum of money which arose from the sale of a negro man named Stephen purchased by the said Gaines from an inhabitant of North Carolina, whence the said negro was brought in the year one thousand eight hundred and twelve, and sold, in consequence thereof, by the overseers of the poor of the county of Charlotte.

2. This act shall be in force from the passing thereof.

1813. Chapter CXXXVI. – An ACT placing certain persons on the Pension List.
(Passed January 19th, 1813)

BE it enacted by the General Assembly, That John Peery, now a resident of the county of Cabell, an old revolutionary soldier, (who was severely wounded and disabled by the British at the battle of Alamance in North Carolina,) shall be placed on the pension list, and receive annually sixty dollars, to be paid as other pensions are paid.

2. And be if further enacted, That Argelon Toone, an old revolutionary soldier, who served during the whole war, and whose constitution has been destroyed by the said service, which has reduced himself and family, consisting of a wife, five daughters and a small son, to great distress, shall be placed on the pension list and receive annually sixty dollars, to be paid as other pensioners are paid.

1813. Chapter CIII. – An ACT concerning Anne H. Knight.
(Passed January 27th, 1813)

WHEREAS it is represented to the General Assembly by Anne H. Knight, that she has been compelled by the cruelty of her husband Walton Knight to abandon the idea of living with him and to throw herself on the mercy of her friends, for protection and support; – that her said husband has since formed an adulterous connection with a woman of infamous character, and does not, in the smallest degree, contribute to the support of maintenance of the said Anne, his wife; --

1. Be it there enacted, That it shall and may be lawful for the said Anne H. Knight, to hold and enjoy such property as she may hereafter acquire, as free from the controul of the said Walton Knight her husband, as if she were an unmarried woman.

2. This act shall be in force from the passing thereof.

1814. Chapter XCVII. – An ACT authorizing the sale of a Tract of Land belonging to the Orphans of Peter Lamkin, deceased.

(Passed January 7, 1814)

WHEREAS it appears to the General Assembly that Colonel Peter Lamkin, late of the county of Lunenburg, deceased, died considerably indebted to the estate of Sharp Lamkin, deceased, of whom the said Peter was executor; and that, for the purpose of paying that debt, it would be more expedient, and less prejudicial to the interests of the orphans of the said Peter Lamkin, to make sale of a certain part of his real estate, than of the slaves belonging to the said orphans:

1. *Be it therefore enacted*, That John Taylor, guardian of Jane Cross Lamkin, William H. Taylor, guardian of Mary Sharp Lamkin, and Edmund F. Taylor, guardian of Elizabeth Lewis Lamkin, which said Jane Cross, Mary Sharp, and Elizabeth Lewis are the orphans of the said Peter Lamkin deceased, shall be and they are hereby authorized and empowered, at such time, upon such terms, and in such manner, as the court of the said county of Lunenburg shall order and direct, to make sale of a tract of unimproved land lying on Flat Rock creek in the said county, belonging to their said wards, and containing between three and four hundred acres, and to convey the same to the purchaser or purchasers thereof in fee simple: *Provided*, that the said John Taylor, William H. Taylor and Edmund F. Taylor, guardians as aforesaid, do and shall, before they proceed to make the sale hereby authorized, enter into bonds with sufficient securities, before the court of the said county of Lunenburg, and payable to the justices thereof then sitting, with condition well and faithfully, as guardians aforesaid, to apply the proceeds arising from such sale, or so much thereof as may be necessary, to the purpose of satisfying and paying the debt aforesaid, due to the estate of the said Sharp Lamkin, deceased, and the residue, if any, for the benefit of their said wards according to law; which bonds shall be entered of record in said court, and in case of default of either of the said guardians, in the performance of the conditions thereof, may be sued upon in like manner as other guardians' bonds, taken [according] to the laws of this commonwealth.

2. This act shall be in force from the passing thereof.

1814. Chapter CII. – An ACT concerning Richard M. Scott, guardian of the Orphans of James E. Marshall.

(Passed January 11, 1814)

WHEREAS it is represented to the General Assembly, that in the summer of one thousand-eight hundred and twelve, James Elgin Marshall of the state of Maryland departed this life, leaving Richard Marshall Scott of the county of Fairfax, in this commonwealth, as his sole executor and guardian of his children; that the said Scott placed his said wards at board and school within the district of Columbia, but considers his house in this state as their home:

1. *Be it therefore enacted*, That it shall and may be lawful for the said Richard M. Scott to bring into this commonwealth the following slaves, to wit: Harry, Walter, Priscilla, Pheda, Henry, Polly, Celia, Lissey, Sarah, Anne, Betty, Milly and Spencer, held by him as guardian of the infant children of the said James E. Marshall, deceased, and to hold them therein in the same manner that he would have been by law authorized, had he have removed his said wards, to his house in this state, at the

time of their father's death.

    2. This act shall be in force from the passing thereof.

1814. Chapter LXXXVI. – An ACT divorcing Elizabeth Robertson from her husband John A. Robertson.

(Passed January 22, 1814)

    1. BE *it enacted by the General Assembly*, That a marriage, solemnized between John A. Robertson of the county of Nottoway, and Elizabeth his wife, shall be and the same is hereby dissolved, and the said Elizabeth forever divorced from the said John A.; and the power of the said John A. over the person and property of the said Elizabeth shall entirely cease.

    2. *Provided nevertheless*, That this act shall not be so construed as to authorize either the said John A. Robertson or Elizabeth Robertson during the lifetime of the other to intermarry with any other person: and if either of them shall so intermarry, he or she so offending shall be deemed guilty of bigamy, and shall be punished in the same manner as if this act had never been passed.

    3. This act shall be in force from the passing thereof.

1814. Chapter XCI. – An ACT concerning Sarah Easton and Dorothy Storer.

(Passed February 9, 1814)

WHEREAS it is represented to the General Assembly, by the memorial and accompanying documents of Sarah Easton and Dorothy Storer, that their father, lieutenant colonel Robert Hanson Harrison deceased, rendered to this State, and to the United States, during the revolutionary war, as one of the aids and as secretary to general George Washington, most "essential service" by discharging the duties of those offices with "conspicuous abilities," and the "strictest integrity," for which neither he in his lifetime, nor his descendants since his death, ever received the depreciation of pay, and the bounty in lands, allowed by the commonwealth to officers from Virginia similarly circumstanced;

    1. *Be it therefore enacted*, That Sarah Easton and Dorothy Storer, the daughters and legal representatives of Robert Hanson Harrison, shall be entitled, in right of their deceased father, to receive the bounty in lands allowed by law to a lieutenant colonel in the State or Continental line of the revolutionary army; and the register of the land office is hereby authorized and required to issue one or more warrants therefor to the said Sarah Easton and Dorothy Storer, or to their legal representatives.

    2. *And be it further enacted*, That the auditor of public accounts shall be and he is hereby authorised and required to settle with the said representatives of Robert Hanson Harrison the depreciation of pay of a lieutenant colonel in the State or Continental line, and issue a warrant on the treasury for the amount which would be due therefor, had the claims of the said Robert Hanson Harrison been recognised and settled in his lifetime, in the same manner and upon the same principles on which the like allowance was made to lieutenant colonel Richard Kidder Meade, another aid of general George Washington.

    3. This act shall be in force from and after the passage thereof.

1814. Chapter CL. – An ACT concerning John Griffith.
(Passed November 9th, 1814)

WHEREAS it is represented to the General Assembly by John Griffith, of the County of Wood, that he has lately removed, from the State of Maryland to his residence in the said County, a negro woman slave, named Molly, which slave he derived by descend from his father; who was formerly a resident of the County of [Berkeley] in this State; and the said John Griffith having petitioned the Legislature to relieve him from the penalty which, through ignorance, he has incurred in failing to have the said slave registered according to law;

1. *Be it enacted*, That the said John Griffith, on his complying within three months after the passage of this act with the provisions of the first section of the act concerning slaves passed the 9th of January eighteen hundred and thirteen, shall be and he is hereby allowed to hold the said slaves as his property within this commonwealth; and all fines, forfeitures or penalties incurred by him in consequence of the failure aforesaid shall be and the same are hereby remitted.

2. This Act shall be in force from the passing thereof.

1814. Chapter CII. – An ACT concerning Mary Andrews.
(Passed November 23d, 1814)

1. *Be it enacted by the General Assembly*, That Mary Andrews of the City of Williamsburg be, and she is hereby permitted to bring into this state the following slaves natives thereof and loaned by her to J.B. Wilkinson and Robert Andrews of the Mississippi Territory, viz.: Zack, Washington, Susan, Sarah and her two children, Billy, John, Priscilla, Mary, Fanny, Hannah and two children, together with their increase if any, and to hold and enjoy the said slaves in like manner as if they had never been permitted to be carried out of the State. – *Provided nevertheless*, That nothing in this act contained shall be so construed as to affect the private rights of any person or persons whatsoever, which may have been acquired by reason of the removal of said slaves, or their increase beyond the limits of this commonwealth.

2. This Act shall be in force from the passing thereof.

1814. Chapter XCVIII. – An ACT divorcing Richard Jones from his wife Peggy.
(Passed November 25th, 1814)

1. BE *it enacted by the General Assembly*, That a marriage solemnized between Richard Jones,[4] of the County of Northampton, and his wife Peggy, shall be and the same is hereby dissolved, and the said Richard forever divorced from the said Peggy; and that the power of the said Richard over the person and property of the said Peggy shall henceforth entirely cease: *Provided*, it shall be found by the verdict of a jury, upon the trial of an issue before the Superior Court of law of Northampton County; which issue is hereby directed to be made up between the said Richard and Peggy, that the child of the said Peggy Jones is not the child of the said Richard Jones, but is the offspring of some man of colour; which jury the Judge of the Superior Court of Law to be holden for the said County of Northampton, at the next term of said Court or as soon thereafter as may be, is hereby authorized and directed

---

[4] Legislative Petition, Northampton Co., November 2, 1814. *Bill Drawn.*

to impanel for the trial of said issue, upon being satisfied that said Peggy Jones had been furnished with a copy of this law, or that said copy had been left at her last and usual place of abode one month before the session of said Court.

2. *Be if further enacted*, That the Supreme Court of law for said County of Northampton shall cause the verdict of the Jury hereby directed to be recorded.

3. *Be it enacted*, That, if the said Jury, so as aforesaid to be impanelled, shall by their verdict find that the child of the said Petty Jones is not the child of said Richard Jones but is the offspring of a man of colour; and if thereafter the said Richard Jones shall die intestate as to all or any part of his real or personal estate, the said child shall not succeed or to enjoy any part thereof.

4. This Act shall be in force from the passing thereof.

1814. Chapter XCIX. – An ACT divorcing Oney Warner from her husband Osborn Warner.
(Passed December 6th, 1814)

1. *Be it enacted by the General Assembly*, That a marriage solemnized between a certain Osborn Warner and his wife Oney, formerly Oney Jourdan, shall be, and the same is hereby dissolved, and the said Oney forever divorced from the said Osborn; and that the power of the said Osborn over the person and property of the said Oney shall henceforth entirely cease.

2. This Act shall be in force from the passing thereof.

1814. Chapter C. – An ACT concerning Susanna Hubard and her infant children.
(Passed December 7th, 1814)

WHEREAS it hath been represented to this present General Assembly by Susanna Hubard, on behalf of herself and her infant children, that of her late husband James T. Hubard in his life time made a purchase of a very valuable tract of land in the County of Buckingham, of Colonel Samuel Allen, one of the trustees named in a marriage settlement entered into prior to her intermarriage with the said James T. Hubard, with the consent of the other trustees in the said marriage contract named; and that the money to be paid for the same should be advanced by the said trustees out of the trust estate, and the said lands settled agreeably to the provisions of the said marriage contract; that, in pursuance of the said agreement, several sums were advanced on account of the said purchase; and that there remains now due a considerable sum, but which is much less than the value of the said tract of land, and that it would be highly beneficial to the persons interested under the said marriage settlement, if a part of the trust estate should be sold to raise the sum necessary, to pay the balance due for the said tract of land;

1. *Be it therefore enacted*, That Charles Yancey, Linnaeus Bolling, Anthony Dibrell and James Walker, or any two or more of them, be, and they are hereby authorized and empowered to make sale of so much of the estate comprehended in the said marriage settlement, either at public auction or private sale, as they may deem most beneficial to the persons interested under the said settlement, as shall be sufficient to pay and satisfy the balance of the purchase money, with interest, due for the said tract of land in the County of Buckingham purchased by the said James T. Hubard in his lifetime as aforesaid, and the expenses of the sale; and after defraying

such expenses, that they pay over, to the person or persons entitled to receive the same, the said balance of the purchase money with interest, and cause and procure a conveyance to be made for the said tract of land to the surviving trustees, named in the said marriage settlement and their heirs, to be by them held upon the same trust, and for the same persons, and upon the same uses as are limited and provided for the other property conveyed in and by the marriage settlement in like manner as if the said tract of land had been included in the said marriage contract.

2. This Act shall be in force from the passing thereof.

1816. Chapter CLIV. – An ACT concerning Frances Smith.
(Passed January 8th, 1816)

1. *Be it enacted by the General Assembly*, That the sum of seventy-three dollars one and a half cents shall be and the same is hereby allowed to Frances Smith widow and administratrix of John Smith, late of the county of York, as compensation for furnishing various articles of provision, during the war, to the officers and soldiers of this State; and the Auditor of Public Accounts is authorized and required to issue a warrant on the Treasury to her, or her representative, for the same, to be paid out of any monies therein not otherwise appropriated.

2. This Act shall be in force from the passing thereof.

1816. Chapter CXXXV. – An ACT authorizing the divorce of Hezekiah Mosby from his wife Betsy.
(Passed January 25th, 1816)

WHEREAS it is represented to the General Assembly, by Hezekiah Mosby, of the county of Powhatan, that he hath intermarried with a certain Betsy Merryman; that he has since faithfully performed the duties of a husband towards the said Betsy; but that she, regardless of her marriage vow, hath been guilty of the crime of adultery, and hath borne a child, the offspring of adulterous intercourse with a man of color; and the said Hezekiah Mosby hath prayed a divorce from his said wife;

1. *Be it therefore enacted*, That it shall be lawful for the said Hezekiah Mosby to exhibit his bill of complaint in the Superior Court of Chancery for the district of Richmond, making his said wife a defendant thereto, calling upon her to answer to the charges aforesaid, and praying a decree of the Court for a divorce from the bonds of matrimony. Upon the coming in of the answer of the said Betsy, whether the allegations of the bill be confessed, denied or evaded, or upon her failure to appear, for three months, after the service of the subpœna, the Court shall direct issues to be made up and tried at the bar of some Superior Court of Law, or at its own bar, to ascertain the following facts: – First, whether the said Hezekiah Mosby hath faithfully performed his duties as a husband towards the said Betsy since their intermarriage; and, secondly, whether the said Betsy hath been guilty of the crime of adultery with a man of color, since her intermarriage with the said Hezekiah. The Court shall also direct an account to ascertain the value and profits of the estate of the said Hezekiah and the amount of property which the said Hezekiah may have obtained by his marriage with the said Betsy. If, upon the trial of the issues aforesaid, it shall be found that the said Betsy hath been guilty of the crime of adultery with a man of color, it shall be the duty of the said Court of Chancery to pronounce a decree, divorcing

24

the said Hezekiah from his wife Betsy; and, from henceforth, the power and authority of the said Hezekiah over the person and property of the said Betsy shall cease. But the said Betsy shall be wholly precluded from the right to intermarry with any other person during the life of the said Hezekiah; and if she offend herein, she shall be liable to all the pains and penalties imposed by law upon the offence of bigamy. And, if it be found, upon the trial of the issues aforesaid, that the said Hezekiah hath not faithfully performed the duties of a husband towards the said Betsy since their intermarriage, then the said Hezekiah, notwithstanding the decree of divorce to be pronounced as aforesaid, shall be wholly precluded from intermarrying with any other person, during the life of the said Betsy; and if he offen therein, he shall be liable to all the pains and penalties imposed by law upon the offence of bigamy. The said Court, on pronouncing a decree of divorce between the said parties, shall allow alimony to the said Betsy, or not, as so the Court shall seem proper; and shall make such other decree in favor of the said Betsy in relation to the property of the said Hezekiah as justice may seem to require. But, if, upon the trial of the issues aforesaid, it shall be found that the said Betsy is not guilty of the offence of adultery with a man of color as aforesaid, then the said bill shall be dismissed.

    2. This Act shall be in force from the passage thereof.

1816. Chapter CLV. – An ACT concerning James Durell.
(Passed January 25th, 1816)

    1. *Be it enacted by the General Assembly*, That the Auditor of Public Accounts is hereby authorized and required to issue a warrant on the Treasury to James Durell of the town of Petersburg, for eight hundred and seventy two dollars, as a compensation for the damages done by the explosion of gun powder to his lumber house, which was impressed and used as a magazine for the use of the militia, stationed in the said town of Petersburg, in the year one thousand eight hundred and fourteen; to be paid out of any monies therein not otherwise appropriated.

    2. This Act shall be in force from the passing thereof.

1816. Chapter CLVI. – An ACT concerning the widow and children of Roger W. Hughlett, deceased.
(Passed January 30th, 1816)

WHEREAS it is represented to the General Assembly, that, early in the month of april, in the year one thousand eight hundred and fourteen, the dwelling house of the late Roger C. Hughlett of the county of Northumberland was, by order of the Lieutenant Colonel Commandant of the thirty seventh Regiment, impressed as barracks for the use of the troops of this State, and occupied as such; that, in the month of October following, the said house was burnt by the enemy, in consequence of its being occupied as barracks; no other house, though several were visited by the enemy, having been destroyed at that time;

    1. *Be it therefore enacted*, That the Auditor of Public Accounts be and he is hereby authorized and required to issue a warrant on the Treasury, in favor of the legal representatives of the said Robert W. Hughlett deceased, for the sum of fifteen hundred dollars, as compensation for the loss aforesaid, to be paid out of any monies

therein not otherwise appropriated.

2. This Act shall be in force from and after the passing thereof.

1816. Chapter CLVII. – An ACT concerning Robert McCandlish.
(Passed January 31st, 1816)

WHEREAS it is represented to the present General Assembly, that Robert McCandlish was appointed and acted as Recorder, in a Court of Enquiry, appointed by general orders, issued from the Adjutant General's Office, under date of the nineteenth of September one thousand eight hundred and fourteen, or the purpose of enquiring into the military conduct of Colonel Burwell Bassett of the sixty eighth Regiment, and that there is no law authorizing the payment of the compensation allowed him by the said Court;

1. *Be it therefore enacted*, That the sum of eighty-one dollars are hereby allowed the said Robert McCandlish; and the Auditor of Public Accounts is required to issue a warrant on the Treasury for the same; to be paid out of any monies therein arising from militia fines.

2. This Act shall be in force from the passing thereof.

1816. Chapter CXXIV. – An ACT authorizing the sale of a Lot of Land belonging to the heirs of Doctor David Dick.
(Passed February 14th, 1816)

WHEREAS it appears to the General Assembly, that the sale of a certain lot [of] land, adjoining the town of Smithfield and in the county of Isle of Wight, belonging to the heirs of Doctor David Dick, deceased, would advance the interest of the said heirs;

1. *Be it therefore enacted*, That the Court of the county of Isle of Wight is hereby authorized and required, at such time, upon such terms, and in such manner, as the said Court shall order and direct, to make sale of and convey, by one or more Commissioners, to the purchasers, in fee simple, a lot of land, adjoining the town of Smithfield in the said county if Isle of Wight, of which Doctor David Dick died seised and possessed; and allot to, and divide the money arising from such sale, between David Dick, Wardrope Dick and Anne Dick, heirs and distributees of the said Doctor David Dick, deceased, and Anne Dick the widow of the said David, in such proportions as they shall deem just and equitable; and the division or allotment aforesaid, made to the said Anne Dick, widow, shall be in lieu, and in full satisfaction, of her dower in the aforesaid lot of land, and be so much as the court shall deem to be equal to the value of her dower estate. And, the said Samuel Dick being a lunatic, the said Court is hereby required, in the manner directed by law, to appoint a committee for the management of the real and personal estate of said Samuel one of the sons of the said David Dick; taking of the said committee bond and security as in other cases of lunacy. And the said committee shall and is hereby authorized and required to [receive], apply to the use of the said lunatic, and account for according to law, the said Samuel's share of the property to be directed to be sold as aforesaid; *provided, however*, that the sale herein mentioned shall not take place until the

county Court of Isle of Wight shall, upon due consideration first had thereon, adjudge that the interest of the said Samuel Dick will be promoted by such sale.

    2. This Act shall be force from the passing thereof.

1817. Chapter 119. – An ACT divorcing Ann P.P. Cowper from her husband William Cowper.

(Passed January 9th, 1817)

    1. *Be it enacted by the General Assembly*, That a marriage solemnized between William Cowper of the county of Isle of Wight, and Anne P.P. his wife, shall be and the same is hereby forever dissolved and annulled, and the said Anne forever divorced from the said William Cowper; and that all the power or authority of the said William Cowper over the person and property of the said Anne, and all the power and authority of the said William Cowper, as guardian by nature, over the persons and property of the children, the off-spring of the said marriage, shall henceforth entirely cease and determine, and the said Anne is hereby restored to all the rights and privileges of a *feme sole*; and the proper court is hereby authorized to appoint a guardian or guardians of the persons and property of said children as if they were orphans: *Provided, however*, That such court shall, in no event, appoint the said William Cowper guardian as aforesaid: *Provided, also*, That nothing in this act contained shall be so construed as to prevent the children aforesaid from inheriting and transmitting inheritance in the same manner as if this act had never been passed; and that nothing herein contained shall be so construed as to authorize either the said Anne P.P. Cowper or William Cowper, during the life time of the other, to intermarry with any other person; and if either of them shall so intermarry, he or she so offending shall be deemed guilty of bigamy, and shall be punished in the same manner as if this act had never passed.

    2. This act shall be in force from the passing thereof.

1816. Chapter 120. – An ACT divorcing Abraham Newton from his wife Nancy.

(Passed January 10th, 1817)

WHEREAS it appears to the General Assembly that, some time in the year eighteen hundred and fifteen, Abraham Newton of the county of Fauquier was married to a certain Nancy Gray; and that, in about five months after the said marriage, the said Nancy was delivered of a mulatto child; and in consideration thereof, the said Abraham having prayed for a divorce;

    1. *Be it enacted by the General Assembly*, That the marriage solemnized between the said Abraham Newton and Nancy Gray shall be, and the same is hereby dissolved, and the said Abraham forever divorced from the said Nancy; and that the proper and authority of the said Abraham over the person and property of the said Nancy shall henceforth entirely cease.

    2. This act shall be in force from the passage thereof.

1817. Chapter 150. – An ACT concerning Lilburn L. Henderson.
(Passed January 23d, 1817)

WHEREAS it is represented to the General Assembly, that, about the year one thousand eight hundred and fourteen, Lilburn L. Henderson of the county of Washington, brought from Tennessee into this State, two valuable family slaves, and exported therefrom six other slaves, under the belief that by so doing he had complied with the law on that subject, and was, in consequence thereof, fully authorized to hold the said two slaves in this commonwealth; and the said Henderson having petitioned the Legislature to be permitted so to hold the said slaves;

1. *Be it enacted*, That the said Lilburn L. Henderson shall be and he is hereby authorized and empowered to hold the said two slaves, known by the names of Taby and Patsy, in this commonwealth, free from any fine, penalty, or forfeiture whatsoever, incurred or to be incurred by reason of his having brought the said slaves into this commonwealth as aforesaid.

2. This act shall be in force from the passage thereof.

1817. Chapter 151. – An ACT for the relief of the heirs of Edward Carter, deceased.
(Passed February 20th, 1817)

WHEREAS it is represented to the General Assembly, that, by a decree of the superior court of chancery held for the district of Fredericksburg, it was ordered that the lands of which Edward Carter late of Prince William county died seized, should be equally divided among his four sons Edward, Cassius, Charles, Shirley and John Hill Carter [sic], and whereas, also, Charles Carter of *Shirley* in his life time conveyed in trust to Robert Randolph a certain tract of land, called *Saints Hill*, adjoining that so devised by the said Edward, to the use and benefit of the said sons of the said Edward, and by the said deed of trust directed that the said tract of land, called *Saints Hill*, should be equally also divided among the said sons of Edward Carter, which trust has by decree of the court aforesaid since been transferred to Thomas Turner, who is the guardian of the sons of the said Edward and has represented to this General Assembly, that to divide both the said tracts according to the said decree and deed of trust would produce a serious inconvenience to the said sons of the said Edward Carter, of holding two small tracts of land in the same neighbourhood, instead of a compact farm to each; to remedy which inconvenience;

1. *Be it enacted*, That Landon Carter, John Carter, John Carter, John Love Washington, John Washington, Griffin Stith, and Ariss Buckner, or any three of them, being the commissioners named in the said decree, lay off and divide the whole land to which the said sons of Edward Carter are entitled under the said decree and deed of trust, as may appear to them best calculated to promote and secure the interests of the said sons of the said Edward Carter, and that the said trustee do, in execution of his trust, convey according to such division.

2. *And be in enacted*, That the act, entitled "An act concerning the children of Edward Carter, deceased," passed the 20th day of February 1816, be and the same is hereby repealed.

3. This act shall be in force from the passing thereof.

28

1817. Chapter 152. – An ACT concerning Hezekiah Starr.

(Passed January 29th, 1817)

WHEREAS it is represented to the General Assembly, by Hezekiah Starr, that, during the last year, he removed from the city of Baltimore to this State, with the intention of residing permanently therein, and brought with him two slaves for his own personal service, without the previous knowledge that such removal of the said slaves was inhibited by the laws of this State; and the said Hezekiah Starr having prayed of the Legislature permission to retain the said slaves therein as his property;

1. *Be it enacted*, That the said Hezekiah Starr shall and he is hereby authorized and empowered to hold in this commonwealth the said two slaves, known by the names of Maria and William, free from any fine, penalty, or forfeiture whatsoever, incurred or to be incurred by reason of their removal into this State as aforesaid; *Provided*, That the said Hezekiah Starr shall, within sixty days from the passage of this act, conform to the requisitions contained in the proviso of the first section of the act, entitled "An act concerning slaves," passed on the 9th day of January 1813, except so far as that act requires an oath that such slaves were not brought into the state in any manner contrary to the provisions of that law.

2. This act shall be in force from and after the passing thereof.

1817. Chapter 153. – An ACT concerning Edward Powell.

(Passed January 29th, 1817)

1. *Be it enacted by the General Assembly*, That the auditor of public accounts is hereby authorized and required to issue a warrant on the treasury for one hundred and ten dollars, and the interest thereon, to Edward Powell of the town of Petersburg, or his representative, as an indemnification for the loss of his horse, impressed in the service of the commonwealth on the 10th day of February in the year 1813, to be paid out of any money therein not otherwise appropriated.

2. This act shall be in force from the passing thereof.

1818. Chapter CCXX. – An ACT divorcing Mary Burke from her husband Michael Burke.

(Passed February 14th, 1818)

WHEREAS it is represented to the General Assembly, that, in the year one thousand eight hundred and fourteen, Mary Burke intermarried with a certain Michael Burke, who, in a short time thereafter, became addicted to the habits of idleness and intemperance, totally destructive of all domestic happiness; that the said Michael Burke proceeded from one rash and vicious step to another, until he committed a most wicked and atrocious murder on the body of his brother-in-law, Thomas Warrell, late of the town of Petersburg, and then fled the country, leaving his wife exposed to all the miseries arising from pecuniary want:

1. *Be it therefore enacted*, That the marriage solemnized between the said Michael Burke and Mary Burke his wife, shall be and the same is hereby dissolved, and the said Mary forever divorced from the said Michael; and that the power and authority of the said Michael Burke over the person and property of the said Mary shall henceforth entirely cease and determine: *Provided*, that nothing herein contained shall be so construed as to authorise either the said Mary or Michael

29

Burke, during the life time of the other, to intermarry with any other person; and, if either of them shall so intermarry, he or she so offending shall be deemed guilty of bigamy, and shall be punished in the same manner as if this act had never been passed.

2. This act shall be in force from the passage thereof.

1818. Chapter CCXXI. – An ACT divorcing Nancy Anderson from her husband William R. Anderson.
(Passed February 10th, 1818)

1. BE *it enacted by the General Assembly*, That a marriage solemnized between William R. Anderson, of the county of Washington, and Nancy his wife, formerly Nancy Conn, shall be and the same is hereby dissolved, and the said Nancy forever divorced from the said William R.; and, that the power and authority of the said William R. over the person and property of the said Nancy, and over the persons and property of the children, the offspring of said marriage, shall henceforth entirely cease: *Provided nevertheless*, that this act shall not be so construed as to authorise either the said William R. or the said Nancy, during the life time of the other, to intermarry with any other person; and, if either of them shall so intermarry, he or she so offending shall be deemed guilty of bigamy, and shall be punished in the same manner as if this act had never been passed: And *provided also*, that nothing in this act contained shall be so construed as to prevent the children of said Nancy Anderson and William R. Anderson from inheriting and transmitting inheritance in the same manner as if this act had never been passed.

2. This act shall be in force from the passage thereof.

1818. Chapter CCXXII. – An ACT divorcing Sopha Dobyns from her husband Jonah Dobyns.
(Passed February 10th, 1818)

1. BE *it enacted by the General Assembly*, That a marriage solemnized between Jonah Dobyns and Sopha Dobyns, formerly Sopha Leftwich, his wife, shall be and the same is hereby dissolved, and the said Sopha forever divorced from the said Jonah; and, that the power and authority of the said Jonah over the person and property of the said Sopha shall henceforth entirely cease and determine, and the said Sopha is hereby restored to all the rights and privileges of a *feme sole*: *Provided*, that nothing in this act contained shall be so construed as to prevent the children of the said Jonah and Sopha from inheriting and transmitting inheritance in the same manner as if this act had never been passed; and that nothing herein contained shall be so construed as to authorise either the said Jonah Dobyns or the said Sopha Dobyns, during the life time of the other, to intermarry with any other person; and, if either of them shall so intermarry, he or she so offending shall be deemed guilty of bigamy, and shall be punished in the same manner as if this act had never passed.

2. This act shall be in force from the passage thereof.

1818. Chapter CCXXIII. – An ACT divorcing Sarah C. Grantham from her husband Uriah Grantham.
(Passed February 26th, 1818)

1. BE *it enacted by the General Assembly*, That a marriage solemnized between Uriah Grantham, of the county of Prince George, and Sarah C. Grantham, his wife, shall be and the same is hereby dissolved, and the said Sarah forever divorced from the said Uriah; and that the power and authority of the said Uriah over the person and property of the said Sarah shall henceforth entirely cease.

2. *Provided nevertheless*, That this act shall not be so construed as to authorise either the said Uriah Grantham or Sarah C. Grantham, during the life time of the other, to intermarry with any other person; and if either the said Uriah or Sarah C. shall so intermarry, he or she shall be deemed guilty of bigamy, and shall be punished in the same manner as if this act had never been passed.

3. This act shall be in force from the passage thereof.

1818. Chapter CCXXIV. – An ACT vesting in Milly Clayton the Commonwealth's right to the real estate of which William Clayton died seized.
(Passed February 7th, 1818)

WHEREAS it is represented to the General Assembly, by Milly Clayton of the Borough of Norfolk, that her late husband William Clayton departed this life some time since, having previously devised a small real estate, which had been acquired by their joint industry, to certain relations of his residing in the West Indies; that she is poor and needy, and that, the persons to whom the said estate was devised being aliens, and incapable under the law of holding the same, the right thereto is now vested in the Commonwealth for the benefit of the Literary Fund; and, the said Milly Clayton having prayed of the Legislature a release of the Commonwealth's right to the said estate in her favor:

1. *Be it enacted*, That all the right, title or interest which hath accrued or may accrue to the Commonwealth, or to the president and directors of the Literary Fund, in or to the real estate of which the said William Clayton died seized, shall be, and the same is hereby vested in the said Milly Clayton; saving however to all persons, bodies politic or corporate, other than the Commonwealth, and the president and directors of the Literary Fund, any right, title or interest, which they might or would have had in or to the said estate, or any part thereof, if this act had not been made.

2. This act shall be in force from the passing thereof.

1819. Chapter CLXII. – An ACT increasing the pension of Edward Houchins.
(Passed January 5th, 1819)

1. BE *it enacted by the General Assembly*, That Edward Houchins of the county of Louisa, an old soldier of the revolution who was severely wounded in the arm at Gates's defeat, shall hereafter receive annually eighty dollars, (instead of forty which he has heretofore received,) to be paid as formerly.

2. This act shall be in force from the passing thereof.

1819. Chapter CXLII. – An ACT authorizing a sale of certain real and personal estate belonging to Lucy Bullock, a lunatic.
(Passed January 8th, 1819)

1. BE *it enacted by the General Assembly*, That George Hamilton, and George M. Buckner, commissioners for that purpose, are hereby empowered and authorized to sell a piece of land lying in [Spotsylvania] county, containing about thirty acres, and one woman slave and her five children, property belonging to Lucy Bullock, a person of insane mind, and convey the same to the purchasers: *Provided*, That the said George Hamilton and George M. Buckner, before they proceed to make sale of the property aforesaid, shall enter into bond with sufficient security, to the justices of Spotsylvania court then sitting, and their successors, conditioned well and faithfully to invest the proceeds of such sales, in such stocks, or loans upon security on real estate, as the said court may direct, and to apply the dividends or interest annually arising from such proceeds so invested or loaned, to the support and maintenance of the said lunatic Lucy Bullock: *And provided also*, That all such charges for advancements for the maintenance and support of the said Lucy Bullock, shall be annually settled and allowed by the court of Spotsylvania, and there recorded.

2. *And be it further enacted*, That the stocks or money loaned, the proceeds of the sale authorized by this act, at the death of the said Lucy Bullock, shall pass and descend in the same manner, and to the same persons, as if this law had not passed.

3. This act shall be in force from and after the passing thereof.

1819. Chapter CLXIII. – An ACT placing Andrew Scidmore on the pension list, and for his present relief.
(Passed January 20th, 1819)

1. BE *it enacted by the General Assembly*, That Andrew Scidmore of the county of Nicholas, an old soldier, who was severely wounded in the hand at Point Pleasant, whilst under the command of Colonel Andrew Lewis in the year seventeen hundred and seventy-four, shall receive sixty dollars for his present relief; and the Auditor of Public Accounts is authorized and required to issue a warrant on the Treasury to him, or William Marteney for his use, for the same, to be paid out of any money therein not otherwise appropriated.

2. *And be it further enacted*, That he shall be placed on the pension list, and receive annually eighty dollars, to be paid as other pensioners are paid.

3. This act shall be in force from the passing thereof.

1819. Chapter CLXI. – An ACT divorcing Maria Brown from her husband Hugh Brown.
(Passed February 3rd, 1819)

1. BE *it enacted by the General Assembly*, That a marriage solemnized between Hugh Brown, formerly of the town of Fredericksburg, and Maria Brown his wife, shall be and the same is hereby dissolved, and the said Maria for ever divorced from the said Hugh; and, that the power and authority of the said Hugh, over the person and property of the said Maria, shall henceforth entirely cease: *Provided,*

nevertheless, that this act shall not be so construed, as to authorize either the said Hugh or the said Maria, during the life time of the other, to intermarry with any other person; and, if either of them shall so intermarry, he or she so offending shall be deemed guilty of bigamy, and shall be punished in the same manner as if this act had never been passed.

2. This act shall be in force from the passage thereof.

1819. Chapter CXLIII. – An ACT authorizing a sale of certain real property belonging to the infant heirs of Jesse Butts, deceased.
(Passed February 3d, 1819)

WHEREAS it is presented to the present General Assembly, that Jesse Butts, late of the county of Greensville, departed this life in the year eighteen hundred and sixteen intestate, leaving five children, three of whom are infants; that the said Jesse was at the time of his death seized of a tract of land containing about three hundred and eighty-two acres, which is nearly divested of wood, and is moreover, much worn; that the commissioners appointed by the county court of Greensville to divide the said land amongst the heirs of the said decedent, refused to act, from a conviction that justice could not be done the parties in such division; and whereas it is also represented that a sale of the said land would be beneficial to all the parties concerned therein:

1. *Be it therefore enacted*, That Edmund Mason, Benjamin Jones, Williamson Bonner, Nathaniel Mabry and Thomas Gibbon, be, and they are hereby appointed commissioners, who, or any three of whom, are hereby authorized and empowered, upon such terms and in such manner, as the court of the county of Greensville shall order and direct, to make sale, in conjunction with the adult distributees of the said Jesse Butts, deceased, of the said infants' interests in the tract of land aforesaid, and convey the same to the purchaser or purchasers thereof in fee. And the money arising from the sale of the said infants' interest in the said land shall, by the said commissioners, be paid over to the guardian or guardians of the said infants, who shall give such additional bond or bonds, as the said court may think necessary for protecting and securing the interests of the said infants; which bond or bonds shall have like force and effect as guardians' bonds taken according to the laws of this Commonwealth.

2. This act shall be in force from the passing thereof.

1819. Chapter CXLIV. – An ACT authorizing a sale of certain real property belonging to the heirs of General John B. Scott, deceased.
(Passed January 15th, 1819)

WHEREAS it appears to the General Assembly, that a sale of a tract of land lying in Halifax county, whereof General John B. Scott died seized and possessed, would greatly promote the interest of the several distributees of the said Scott, (a number of whom are infants,) inasmuch as an equitable division of said land cannot be made:

1. *Be it therefore enacted*, That William T. Scott, guardian of Martha Ann Scott, Christopher C. Scott and Elizabeth R. Scott; John W. Scott, guardian of James B. Scott and Francis T. Scott, shall be, and they are hereby authorized and empowered, upon such terms, and in such manner as the court of the county of

Halifax shall order and direct, if the said county court of Halifax, upon due deliberation, shall be of opinion that the interest of the said infant distributees or heirs of the said General John B. Scott will be promoted by such sale, to make sale in conjunction with the other distributees of said decedent, of the said tract of land whereof the said General John B. Scott died seized, and to convey to the purchaser or purchasers thereof, all the interest of their said wards therein: *Provided, however,* That the said William T. Scott and John W. Scott, shall not be authorized by any think herein contained, to sell the interest of their said wards in the said property, until they shall have entered into bond with good security, to be approved by the said court, in such penalty as the said court shall direct, conditioned for the faithful application of the said proceeds according to law, and for the benefit of their said wards: which bond shall be entered of record in the said court, and in case of default of the said guardians, or either of them, in the performance of the condition thereof, may be sued upon as other guardians' bonds taken according to the laws of this Commonwealth: *Provided,* if the said infant distributees or heirs, or either of them, should die under the age of twenty-one years, the part allotted to such as die, shall pass and descend as the said real estate, whereof the said General John B. Scott died seized, would have descended if this act had never passed; and be subject to all the other legal and equitable rules of real estate: *And provided also,* That no sale shall be directed by the said county court of Halifax, until a summons shall have issued and been served upon the infant distributees or heirs of the said General John B. Scott, and their respective guardians, to shew the cause, if any they, or either of them choose, against such sale.

2. This act shall commence and be in force from and after the passage thereof.

1820. Chapter 116. – An ACT concerning William Walker, administrator of John S. Walker, deceased.

(Passed December 21st, 1820)

1. *Be it enacted by the General Assembly,* That the sum of six hundred dollars is hereby allowed to William Walker, administrator of John S. Walker, deceased, as an indemnification for the loss of a negro man slave, the property of the said decedent, (who was condemned to die in the month of October eighteen hundred and nineteen, by the county court of Cumberland, and valued at the sum aforesaid by the said court; but whose sentence was changed to transportation by the executive, and who broke jail and made his escape;) to be by him accounted for as part of the personal estate of the said decedent; and the auditor of public accounts is hereby authorised and required to issue a warrant on the treasury for the said sum of six hundred dollars, to the said William Walker, administrator as aforesaid, to be paid out of any monies therein not otherwise appropriated.

2. This act shall be in force from the passing thereof.

1820. Chapter CXXIX. – An ACT vesting in Polly and Nathaniel Kelly, children of John Kelly, the Commonwealth's right to certain property therein mentioned.

(Passed February 11th, 1820)

WHEREAS it is represented to the present General Assembly, by John Kelly, that a certain Matthias Simmet, late of the county of Greenbrier, died intestate, seized of certain lands and tenements in the said county, which, as the said Simmet left no relative in this country, are now escheatable to the Commonwealth: and, whereas it is also represented, that the said Simmet, who resided a long time previous to his death in the family of the said Kelly, was frequently heard to declare, that Polly and Nathaniel Kelly, children of the said John Kelly, should, at his death, possess the whole of his estate; and the said John Kelly having petitioned the Legislature to release the Commonwealth's right to the said property, and to confirm in his said children the title thereto:

1. *Be it enacted*, That all the right, title and interest which hath accrued, or may accrue to the Commonwealth, or to the president and directors of the literary fund, in or to the real estate of which the said Matthias Simmet died seized and possessed, shall be, and the same is hereby vested in the said Polly and Nathaniel Kelly, children of the said John Kelly: saving, however, to all persons, bodies politic or corporate, other than the Commonwealth, or the president and directors of the literary fund, any right, title or interest which they might or would have had, in or to the said estate, or any part thereof, if this act had not been made.

2. This act shall be in force from the passing thereof.

1820. Chapter CXXX. – An ACT authorising a sale of certain slaves belonging to the estate of Doctor Robert Berkeley, deceased.

(Passed January 13th, 1820)

WHEREAS it is represented to the present General Assembly, by Julia Berkeley, widow and administratrix of Doctor Robert Berkeley, late of the county of Frederick, deceased, that her said late husband was murdered by his slaves, on his farm in the said county, in the year eighteen hundred and eighteen, under circumstances of the most frightful and appalling barbarity; that three of the said slaves have been capitally punished, and many more of them were evidently implicated in the said murder; that no person is willing to hire them for any thing like a reasonable price, because of the odium justly attached to them; and the said Julia and her infant children, who behold in them the murderers of their husband and father, are apprehensive of meeting a fate as sanguinary and mournful as that which their beloved relative and protector suffered: and the said Julia Berkeley having petitioned the Legislature that a sale of the slaves belonging to the estate of the said Doctor Robert Berkeley, deceased, which were on his farm in the county of Frederick at the time of his decease, and the increase of the females, may be authorised by law;

1. *Be it enacted*, That the said Julia Berkeley, administratrix of the said Doctor Robert Berkeley, deceased, shall be, and she is hereby authorised and empowered, upon such terms, and in such manner as she may think best, to make sale of such slaves belonging to the estate of her said late husband, as were on his farm in the county of Frederick, at the time of his deceased, together with the increase of the

females; the proceeds of which sale to remain in the hands of the said administratrix, subject to the same legal demands, and liable to the same distribution to which the said slaves are now by law subject and liable; and the interest arising or to arise therefrom, to be appropriated in like manner as the hire of said slaves is now by law appropriated: *Provided, however*, That the said Julia Berkeley, administratrix as aforesaid, or some other responsible person, do, and shall, before she proceed to make the sale hereby authorised, enter into bond with sufficient security, before the chancery court for the district of Winchester, or before the judge thereof in vacation, payable to the said judge, and his successors in office, with condition well and faithfully to administer and distribute the proceeds aforesaid, according to the provisions of this act, and of the act or acts for the distribution of intestates' estates: which bond shall be entered of record in the said court; and, in case of default of the said administratrix in the performance of the conditions thereof, may be sued upon in like manner as other administrator's bonds taken according to the laws of this Commonwealth.

2. This act shall be in force from the passing thereof.

1820. Chapter CXXXI. – An ACT divorcing Barbara W. Pettus from Hugh M. Pettus, her husband.

(Passed February 12th, 1820)

1. *Be it enacted by the General Assembly*, That a marriage solemnized between Hugh M. Pettus and Barbara W. Pettus, formerly Barbara W. Price, his wife, shall be, and the same is hereby dissolved, and the said Barbara forever divorced from the said Hugh; and that the power and authority of the said Hugh over the person and property of the said Barbara shall henceforth cease: *Provided*, nevertheless, That the said Hugh shall be wholly precluded from the right to intermarry with any other person during the life of the said Barbara; and, if he offend herein, he shall be liable to all the pains and penalties imposed by law on the offence of bigamy.

2. This act shall be in force from the passing thereof.

1820. Chapter CXXXII. – An ACT divorcing Mary Brady from her husband Thornton Brady.

(Passed February 15th, 1820)

WHEREAS it appears to the present General Assembly, that Mary Brady, formerly Mary Edrington, was deluded into matrimony by her husband Thornton Brady, under the cloak of religion; that, immediately after their marriage, he threw off his mask, became extremely dissipated, cruel and abandoned, even to the commission of adultery in the bed of his said wife; that he has left her and her child, gone to the western country, and there endeavored to marry another woman:

1. *Be it therefore enacted by the General Assembly*, That a marriage solemnized between the said Thornton Brady and Mary his wife, formerly Mary Edrington, shall be, and the same is hereby dissolved, and the said Mary forever divorced from the said Thornton; and that the power and authority of the said Thornton over the person and property of the said Mary, shall henceforth entirely cease: *Provided, nevertheless*, That this act shall not be so construed as to authorise

36

the said Thornton, during the lifetime of the said Mary, to intermarry with any other person; and, if he shall so intermarry, he shall be deemed guilty of bigamy, and shall be punished in the same manner as if this act had never been passed.

2. This act shall be in force from the passing thereof.

1820. Chapter CXXXIII. – An ACT authorising Aggy, a woman of color, to reside within this Commonwealth.
(Passed January 29th, 1820)

WHEREAS it is represented to the present General Assembly, by Charles Cousins, a free man of color of the county of Nottoway, that about eighteen years ago he married a woman of color named Aggy, who, in a short time thereafter was sold under a decree of the county court of Amelia, and purchased by a certain Thomas Howlett for the said Charles Cousins; and in the year eighteen hundred and twelve, he, the said Cousins, repaid to the said Howlett the purchase money so paid for his said wife: that the said Charles Cousins has children by a former marriage, who, in the event of his dying suddenly, would, under the existing laws, become the owners of his said wife; to prevent which, he is anxious for her immediate emancipation, and hath petitioned the Legislature, upon her being emancipated, to extend to her the privilege of remaining in this state:

1. *Be it therefore enacted*, That, when the said Charles Cousins shall have regularly emancipated the said Aggy, she shall be, and is hereby permitted to remain as a free person within this Commonwealth, and to have and enjoy all the rights and privileges which other free persons of color possess and enjoy within the same; any law to the contrary notwithstanding.

2. This act shall be in force from the passing thereof.

1820. Chapter CLVIII. – An ACT authorising Henry Hill to assume the surname of Newman.
(Passed February 22d, 1820)

1. *Be it enacted*, That Henry Hill of the county of Orange, shall be, and he is hereby authorised and empowered to assume the surname of Newman; by which name, when so assumed, he shall be known and called, as his legal and proper name.

2. This act shall be in force from and after the passing thereof.

1820. Chapter CLIII. – An ACT changing the names of Dorothy Jones and Polly Jones.
(Passed February 5th, 1820)

1. *Be it enacted by the General Assembly*, That Dorothy Jones and Polly Jones, daughters of Henry Harrison, of Nansemond, shall hereafter be called and known by the names of Dorothy Jones Harrison and Polly Jones Harrison.

2. This act shall be in force form the passing thereof.

1820. Chapter CLV. – An ACT concerning John Nicholas.
(Passed February 26th, 1820)

WHEREAS it is represented to the General Assembly, by the memorial and accompanying documents of John Nicholas of the county of Buckingham, that, during the revolution, the said John Nicholas was in the military service of the United States, as captain of infantry in the Virginia line, on state establishment, in which service he continued from the first of January in the year seventeen hundred and seventy seven, to the fifth of June in the year seventeen hundred and eighty, when he received a commission of lieutenant colonel of a body of militia raised by this state for the defence of South Carolina, under which commission he continued in the military service of this state, until after the siege of York: And, whereas it appears to the General Assembly, that, during the periods aforesaid, the said John Nicholas rendered faithful, essential and honorable service to this state and the United States, and that he hath never received the depreciation of pay, to which he was by law entitled, for his services from the said first of January 1777, to the fifth of June 1780:

1. *Be it therefore enacted*, That the auditor of public accounts shall be, and he is hereby authorised to settle with the said John Nicholas, his depreciation of pay as a captain of infantry, from the said first day of January 1777, to the fifth day of June 1780, and to grant him a warrant therefor on the treasury, to be paid out of any monies therein not otherwise appropriated.

2. This act shall be in force from the passing thereof.

1821. Chapter 123. – An ACT appointing commissioners to divide certain lands belonging to the heirs of William Moore, deceased.
(Passed January 23d, 1821)

WHEREAS it is represented to the General Assembly, that William Moore, late of the county of Patrick, died in the year eighteen hundred and nineteen, intestate, leaving nine children, who are entitled to considerable landed estate, both in North Carolina and Virginia; that the said lands, if divided in pursuance of the existing laws of the states aforesaid, are liable to be divided into eighteen parts, which would be injurious to the interests of the parties concerned therein:

1. *Be it therefore enacted*, That the court of the county of Patrick, shall be and is hereby authorised and empowered, to appoint four or more commissioners, any three of whom shall have power, in conjunction with commissioners to be appointed for that purpose in the state of North Carolina, to lay off and divide the whole of the lands belonging to the heirs of the said William Moore, deceased, in such manner as in the opinion of the said commissioners will most promote the interest of all the partes concerned therein. And the said commissioners to be appointed by the county court of Patrick, shall return a report of their proceedings as commissioners aforesaid, to the court of the said county of Patrick, there to be recorded.

2. This act shall be in force from the passing thereof.

1821. Chapter 127. – An ACT releasing to John Fergusson the Commonwealth's right to certain lands therein mentioned.

(Passed January 19th, 1821)

WHEREAS it is represented to the General Assembly by John Fergusson, that his mother, who was a native of Virginia, went over to Scotland before the revolutionary war; where he was born and educated; that, having numerous relatives resident in this country, he removed hither and purchased a tract of land in the county of Henrico in this state, with the intention of settling himself permanently thereon; and doubts having arisen as to the ability of the said John Fergusson to hold real estate, he hath petitioned the legislature to pass an act releasing to him the Commonwealth's right to the land purchased as aforesaid:

1. *Be it therefore enacted*, That all right, title, or interest which hath accrued, or may accrue to the Commonwealth, or to the president and directors of the Literary Fund, in or to the tract of land aforesaid, by reason of the alienage of the said John Fergusson, shall be, and the same is hereby released to him, the said John Fergusson; *Provided*, That the said Fergusson, within the space of five years from the passing of this act, shall have taken the measures provided by the laws of the United States for naturalizing an alien: saving however, to all persons, bodies politic or corporate, other than the Commonwealth, and the president and directors of the Literary Fund, any right, title, or interest which they might or would have had in or to the said tract of land, if this act had not been made.

2. This act shall be in force from the passage thereof.

1821. Chapter 128. – An ACT releasing to Margaret Gray the Commonwealth's right to certain real estate therein mentioned.

(Passed February 3d, 1821)

WHEREAS it is represented to the General Assembly, that Margaret Gray, wife of Joseph Gray, of the county of Botetourt, is the daughter and only representative of William Blain, deceased, late of the said county; that the said William Blain emigrated from Ireland to the United States about forty years ago, leaving a wife and one other daughter in that country, where they still reside; that the said Joseph Gray has been regularly admitted a citizen of the United States; and that the said William Blain departed this life in the year eighteen hundred and nineteen, intestate, seized and possessed of certain real estate in the said county of Botetourt, which as the said Margaret has never been naturalized, is now supposed liable to escheat to the Commonwealth: and the said Joseph Gray, and Margaret his wife, having petitioned the legislature to release to them the Commonwealth's right to the said real estate;

1. *Be it enacted*, That all the right, title or interest which hath accrued or may accrue to the Commonwealth, or to the president and directors of the literary fund, in or to the real estate aforesaid, whereof the said William Blain died seized and possessed, shall be, and the same is hereby released to the said Margaret Gray; saving, however, to all persons, bodies politic and corporate ...

1822. Chapter 108. – An ACT authorising the divorce of Rebecca Sims.

(Passed February 28, 1822)

WHEREAS, it is represented to the present General Assembly by Rebecca Sims, that a marriage was lately solemnised, between herself and Hugh S. Sims, of the county of Augusta, and that the said Hugh S. Sims at the time of the ceremony was incapable of consummating the marriage, by reason of natural impotency, which disability he fraudulently concealed from the said Rebecca, whereof the said Rebecca has produced some corroborating proofs, and hath prayed for a divorce from the said Hugh S. Sims; and whereas such fraud, if satisfactorily proved, should be regarded as rendering the said marriage null and void, and doubts are entertained whether any tribunal of justice within this commonwealth, has legal cognizance of said fraud, and competent authority to declare the said marriage void; for remedy whereof,

1. *Be it enacted*, That it shall be lawful for the said Rebecca Sims, by her next friend, to exhibit her bill in equity in the superior court of chancery for the Staunton district, or in any other superior court of chancery in this commonwealth, within whose jurisdiction the said Hugh S. Sims may be, alledging the cause of divorce aforesaid, and praying that the said marriage may be declared null and void; and that she may be forever divorced from the bonds thereof; and it shall be lawful, for the court to proceed in the prosecution and trial of the said bill, according to the accustomed rules, in other chancery causes; and especially to proceed by publication against the said Hugh S. Sims, if he should leave the commonwealth, or should so abscond or conceal himself that the ordinary process cannot be served upon him. It shall also be lawful, for the court to direct such issue of fact, or cause such inspection to be made, as may be deemed proper to ascertain the truth of the charge aforesaid; and ultimately, if the said charge shall be satisfactorily proved, it shall be lawful for the court to declare the marriage aforesaid null and void, and divorce the said Rebecca Sims forever from the bonds thereof; and to award full costs against the said Hugh S. Sims. But if the said charge shall not be established to the satisfaction of the court, the bill shall be dismissed, and double costs shall be awarded to the defendant against the next friend of the plaintiff.

2. This act shall be in force from the passage thereof.

1822. Chapter 100. – An ACT concerning James Keenan, administrator of William Keenan, deceased.

(Passed December 28th, 1822)

WHEREAS, it is represented to the present General Assembly by James Keenan, administrator of William Keenan, deceased, that the said decedent, in his life time, took with him on a voyage from the island of St. Eustatia to the island of St. Thomas in the West Indies, three slaves, to wit: Lavington, Philip and Nelson: that, in the prosecution of the voyage aforesaid, the said William Keenan was murdered by the crew of the vessel in which he sailed, and the said slaves were brought into this commonwealth; and the said James Keenan, administrator as aforesaid, having petitioned the legislature to remit all fines and forfeitures which may have been incurred by the introduction of the said slaves into the state as aforesaid;

1. *Be it enacted*, That all fines, penalties and forfeitures whatsoever, which may have been incurred by the introduction of the said three slaves into this

commonwealth, shall be and the same are hereby remitted: *Provided, however*, That the said James Keenan, administrator as aforesaid, shall, within six months, to be computed from the passage of this act, cause the said three slaves to be removed beyond the limits of this commonwealth.

2. This act shall commence and be in force from and after the passage thereof.

1823. Chapter 98. – An ACT releasing to Moses Parker, James Parker, John Parker, and Sally Ramsey, the commonwealth's right to a tract of land therein mentioned.

(Passed January 6th, 1823)

WHEREAS, it is represented to the present General Assembly, that James Orrey, a native of Great Britain, who became a resident of this State, previous to the year seventeen hundred and sixty-seven, departed this life some years ago, after having made a will, wherein he devised to Moses Parker, James Parker and Nancy Parker, his natural children, a tract of land lying on the side of the Blue Ridge mountain, in the county of Bedford, containing two hundred and six acres: That, the said will not being recorded in consequence of carelessness of a certain Christopher Sutton, now deceased, into whose hands it was placed for safe keeping, the land aforesaid has escheated to the commonwealth: and the said Moses and James Parker, and John Parker, and Sally Ramsey, (the said John and Sally being the children of the aforesaid Nancy Parker, now dead,) having petitioned the legislature, to release to them the commonwealth's right to the land aforesaid:

1. *Be it enacted*, That all the right, title or interest, which hath accrued or may accrue to the commonwealth, or to the president and directors of the Literary Fund, in or to the tract of land aforesaid, whereof the said James Orrey died seized, shall be and the same is hereby released to the said Moses Parker, James Parker, John Parker and Sally Ramsey, in such proportions as they would have been entitled to, if the said Moses, James and Nancy Parker had been the legitimate children of the said James Orrey: saving however, to all persons, bodies politic and corporate, other than the commonwealth, and the president and directors of the Literary Fund, any right, title or interest, which they might or would have had, in or to the said tract of land, or any part thereof, if this act had not been made.

2. This act shall be in force from the passage thereof.

1824. Chapter 94. – An ACT divorcing Tabitha T. Toler from William B. Toler, her husband.

(Passed January 14th, 1824)

1. *Be it enacted by the General Assembly*, That a marriage solemnized between William B. Toler and Tabitha T. Toler his wife, formerly Tabitha T. Carroll, shall be and the same is hereby dissolved, and the said Tabitha forever divorced from the said William; and that the power and authority of the said William over the person and property of the said Tabitha, shall henceforth entirely cease and determine.

2. *And be it further enacted*, That the said Tabitha T. Toler shall be and she is hereby authorised to resume the name of Tabitha T. Carroll; by which name, when

resumed, she shall be known and called as her legal and proper name.

3. This act shall be in force from the passing thereof.

1824. Chapter 102. – An ACT releasing to the children of John McCreery and Mary his wife, the Commonwealth's right to a certain lot of land.

(Passed March 4th, 1824)

WHEREAS it is represented to the General Assembly by John McCreery, that George Magee a native of Ireland, died in the year eighteen hundred and fifteen, in the town of Petersburg, possessed of some personal estate, and a small lot with a lumber-house thereon in the said town, devising the said lot and lumber-house to his brother Andrew Magee, and directing that, in case that [his] brother should die intestate, the said house and lot should go equally to his brother John Magee, and the children of the said McCreery and Mary his wife: that the said Andrew Magee did die intestate; and the said John Magee, who was an alien, is also dead, having never been in this country: that the said McCreery and his children, are the only relatives of the testator George Magee in this country; and strong reasons exist inducing the belief, that if he could have anticipated the deaths of both his brothers, instead of a moiety of the said house and lot, he would have devised the whole thereof to the children of the said McCreery, who were the objects of his particular regard: and the said John McCreery having petitioned the Legislature to release to them the Commonwealth's right and interest in the said house and lot:

1. *Be it enacted*, That all the right, title and interest, which hath accrued or may accrue to the Commonwealth, or to the president and directors of the Literary Fund, in or to the lot and house aforesaid, or any part thereof, shall be and the same is hereby released to the children of the said John McCreery and Mary his wife; saving, however, to all persons, bodies politic and corporate, other than the Commonwealth, and the president and directors of the Literary Fund, any right, title, or interest, which they might or would have had, in or to the said lot and house, or any part thereof, if this act had not been passed.

2. This act shall be in force from the passage thereof.

1825. Chapter 106. – An ACT divorcing Evelina Roane from her husband Newman B. Roane.

(Passed January 12th, 1825)

1. *Be it enacted by the General Assembly*, That Evelina Roane, wife of Newman B. Roane of the county of King William, shall be, and she is hereby, forever divorced from the said Newman B. and the power and authority of the said Newman B. over the person and property of the said Evelina, and over the person and property of the child or children of the said Evelina, shall henceforth entirely cease and determine. But nothing in this act contained shall be so construed as to authorise the said Newman B. during the life of the said Evelina, to intermarry with any other person, or to release him from the bond of matrimony; or, to prevent the child or children, born of the marriage solemnized between the said Newman B. and the said Evelina, from inheriting and transmitting inheritance, in the same manner as if this act had never passed.

2. This act shall be in force from the passing thereof.

1825. Chapter 107. – An ACT divorcing Pamelia B. Cole from her husband John Cole.
(Passed February 4th, 1825)

1. *Be it enacted by the General Assembly*, That Pamelia B. Cole of the county of Chesterfield, wife of John Cole of the said county, shall be, and she is hereby forever divorced from the bed and board of her said husband; and that al the rights and authority of the said John over the person and property of the said Pamelia and her children, be forever abolished: *Provided*, That nothing in this act contained, shall be so construed as to authorise either the said Pamelia, or the said John, during the life of the other, to intermarry with any other person, or to prevent the children born of the marriage solemnized between the said John and the said Pamelia B. from inheriting and transmitting inheritance, in the same manner as if this act had never passed.

2. This act shall be in force from the passing thereof.

1825. Chapter 108. – An ACT divorcing Elizabeth Mills from her husband Martin L. Mills.
(Passed February 12th, 1825)

1. *Be it enacted by the General Assembly*, That Elizabeth Mills of the county of Albemarle, wife of Martin L. Mills, shall be, and she is hereby forever divorced from the bed and board of the said Martin L.; and the power and authority of the said Martin L. over the person and property of the said Elizabeth, and over the person and property of the child or children of the said Elizabeth, shall henceforth entirely cease and determine. But nothing in this act contained, shall be so construed as to prevent the child or children born of the marriage solemnized between the said Martin L. and the said Elizabeth, from inheriting, and transmitting inheritance, in the same manner as if this act had never passed, or to authorise the said Elizabeth, or the said Martin, during the life of the other, to intermarry with any other person.

2. This act shall be in force from the passing thereof.

1826. Chapter 124. – An ACT concerning the heirs of Thomas Carter, deceased.
(Passed February 23d, 1826)

1. *Be it enacted by the general assembly*, That the Auditor of Public Accounts be, and he is hereby authorised and required to settle with James Broadnax Carter, John Michell Carter, Rebecca Broadnax Standard, (formerly Carter,) Jane Maria Carter and William Boyd, in right of his wife Lucy Gray Edmunds Boyd, (formerly Carter,) the heirs and representatives of Thomas Carter, deceased, the commutation of full pay for five years, in lieu of half pay for life, of the said Thomas Carter as surgeon in the revolutionary war on State establishment; and to issue a warrant on the treasury for the amount, in favor of the said heirs and representatives of the said Carter, to be paid out of any money therein not otherwise appropriated: *Provided*, That nothing in this act shall be so construed as to authorise any payment of interest on the said depreciation of pay, or commutation of half pay, which may be found due for the services of the said Thomas Carter, surgeon as aforesaid.

2. This act shall commence and be in force, from the passing thereof.

1826. Chapter 125. – An ACT concerning the executrix and executors of John Russell, deceased.

(Passed January 13th, 1826)

1. *Be it enacted by the general assembly*, That the Auditor of Public Accounts shall be, and he is hereby authorised and required to settle with Hannah Russell, executrix, and James L. Russell, Gervas E. Russell, Joshua Russell and John B. Russell, executors of John Russell, deceased, or the survivor or survivors of them, the commutation of full pay for five years, in lieu of half pay for life of the said John Russell, deceased, as a lieutenant of infantry in the Virginia line on State establishment, during the revolutionary war, and to issue a warrant on the treasury in favor of the said Hannah Russell, executrix, and James L. Russell, Gervas E. Russell, Joshua Russell and John B. Russell, executors of the said John Russell, deceased, to be paid out of any money therein, not otherwise appropriated: *Provided*, That nothing in this act shall be so construed, as to authorise any payment of interest on the commutation of half pay which may be found due.

2. This act shall commence and be in force, from the passing thereof.

1826. Chapter 132. – An ACT authorising Jeremiah Jeffries, of the county of Westmoreland, to solemnize the Rites of Marriage in the said county.

(Passed March 7th, 1826)

WHEREAS it appears to this General Assembly, that a certain portion of the county of Westmoreland is destitute of a resident Minister, and that they have no person among them authorised to solemnize the rites of marriage:

1. *Be it therefore enacted*, That Jeremiah Jeffries, of the county aforesaid, is hereby authorised to solemnize the rites of marriage in the said county of Westmoreland: *Provided, nevertheless*, That nothing herein contained, shall be so construed, as to change, alter or amend any of the provisions of an act "concerning the solemnization of marriages," passed March the first, eighteen hundred and nineteen; but the said Jeremiah Jeffries shall be, and is hereby possessed of all the powers and subject to all the penalties prescribed by the act aforesaid, for the government of regularly ordained Ministers of the Gospel.

2. This act shall be in force from the passage thereof.

1826. Chapter 133. – An ACT divorcing Ishmael Moody from his wife Eliza Ann.

(Passed February 13th, 18226)

WHEREAS it appears to the General Assembly, that on the twelfth day of March, eighteen hundred and twenty-two, a marriage was solemnized between Ishmael Moody, of the county of Isle of Wight, and a woman calling herself Eliza Ann Eager, but who was in fact at that time the wife of a certain Matthew Hopper, of the State of New York; of which fact, the said Ishmael Moody was entirely ignorant: Therefore, on the petition of the said Ishmael:

1. *Be it enacted*, That the marriage solemnized as aforesaid, between the said Ishmael Moody and the said Eliza Ann Eager, otherwise called Eliza Ann Hopper, otherwise called Catharine Hopper, be dissolved; that the parties aforesaid, be forever divorced, and that all claim and demand of the said Eliza Ann, otherwise called Catharine, in or to the estate, real or personal, of the said Ishmael, henceforth

entirely cease.

2. This act shall be in force from the passage thereof.

1826. Chapter 134. – An ACT divorcing John A. Foulkes from his wife Mary.
(Passed February 16th, 1826)

1. *Be it enacted by the General Assembly*, That John A. Foulkes, formerly of the county of Halifax, in this Commonwealth, shall be, and he is hereby absolutely and entirely, to all intents and purposes, divorced from his wife Mary, formerly Mary Vaughan; and that all right, interest or claim of the said Mary, in or to the estate, real or personal, of the said John, or any part thereof, shall cease and determine, henceforth and forever.

2. This act shall be in force from the passing thereof.

1826. Chapter 135. – An ACT divorcing Amelia M. Alexander from her husband John Alexander.
(Passed February 22d, 1826)

1. *Be it enacted by the General Assembly*, That Amelia M. Alexander of the county of Frederick, wife of John Alexander, shall be, and she is hereby forever divorced from the bed and board of her said husband; and that all the rights and authority of the said John over the person and property of the said Amelia M. be forever abolished: *Provided*, That nothing in this act contained shall be so construed, as to authorise either the said Amelia M. or the said John, during the life of the other, to intermarry with any other person; or to prevent the children born of the marriage solemnized between the said John, and the said Amelia M. from inheriting and transmitting inheritance in the same manner, as if this act had never passed.

2. This act shall be in force from the passage thereof.

1826. Chapter 136. – An ACT divorcing Rachael Cauffman from her husband Simon Cauffman.
(Passed February 24th, 1826)

1. *Be it enacted by the General Assembly*, That Rachael Cauffman of the city of Richmond, shall be, and she is hereby forever divorced from her husband Simon Cauffman: and the power and authority of the said Simon, over the person and property of the said Rachael, and over the persons and property of the children of the said Rachael, shall henceforth cease and determine: *Provided, however*, That nothing in this act contained shall be so construed as to prevent the children of the marriage solemnized between the said Simon and Rachael, from inheriting and transmitting inheritance in the same manner, as if this act had never passed; and provided that nothing herein contained shall be so construed, as to permit either the said Rachael or the said Simon Cauffman, to marry during the life-time the other.

2. This act shall be in force from the passage thereof.

1826. Chapter 137. – An ACT divorcing John Wilson from his wife Patty.
(Passed February 24th, 1826)

1. *Be it enacted by the General Assembly*, That a marriage solemnized between John Wilson of the county of Berkeley, and Patty his wife, formerly Patty Whitlock, shall be, and the same is hereby dissolved, and the said John forever divorced from the said Patty: *Provided*, That nothing herein contained shall be so construed as to authorise either of the said parties to marry, during the life-time of the other.

2. This act shall be in force from the passage thereof.

1827. Chapter 112. – An ACT to change the name of Thomas W. M'Cormick.
(Passed January 3d, 1827)

1. BE *it enacted by the General Assembly*, That the surname of Thomas Winston M'Cormick, the adopted son of John Johns, of the county of Buckingham, shall be changed to Johns, and that his legal and proper name shall hereafter be Thomas Winston Johns.

2. This act shall commence and be in force from and after its passage.

1827. Chapter 137. – An ACT divorcing Macy alias Amasa Gay, from her husband Charles Gay.
(Passed January 25th, 1827)

1. *Be it enacted by the general assembly*, That the marriage heretofore solemnized between Charles Gay, formerly of the county of Sussex, but now of the State of North Carolina, and Macy alias Amasa, his wife, formerly Macy alias Amasa Birdsong, who still resides in the said county of Sussex, shall be, and the same is hereby dissolved, and the said Macy alias Amasa, forever divorced from the said Charles; and the power and authority of the said Charles over the person and property of the said Macy alias Amasa, shall henceforth cease and determine: *Provided nevertheless*, That nothing in this act contained, shall be so construed as to authorise the said Charles Gay to marry any person or persons, the said Macy alias Amasa being alive; but the said Charles Gay, if (after the passage of this act, and during the life of the said Macy,) he shall marry any person or persons, shall be subject to the same pains, penalties and punishment, to which he would have been subject had this act never been passed.

2. This act shall be in force from the passage thereof.

1827. Chapter 138. – An ACT divorcing David Parker from his wife Jane.
(Passed January 17th, 1827)

1. *Be it enacted by the general assembly*, That David Parker, of the county of Nansemond, shall be, and he is hereby absolutely, and entirely, to all intents and purposes, divorced from his wife Jane, formerly Jane Miller; and that all right, interest or claim of said Jane, in or to the estate, real or personal, of the said David, or any part thereof, shall cease and determine henceforth and forever: *Provided however*, That if the said Jane shall hereafter marry during the life of the said David Parker, she shall be subject to all the pains and penalties of bigamy, in the same manner as if this

act had never passed.

2. This act shall be in force from the passage thereof.

1827. Chapter 113. – An ACT concerning William Lynch.

(Passed February 9th, 1827)

WHEREAS it is represented to the General Assembly, that William Lynch, senior, of the county of Brunswick, is the father of thirty-four legitimate children, of whom twenty-seven are now living; that he has been the husband of four wives, the last of whom is now young and healthy and gives him every assurance of an increase of his numerous progeny; that he was a soldier in the war of the revolution, and has been through life, an upright and useful citizen; but that age and the support of his numerous family, have at length rendered him infirm and poor:

1. *Be it enacted by the General Assembly*, That William Lynch of the county of Brunswick, shall be hereafter exempt from the payment of any public or county tax, levy, charge or contribution whatever; and it shall not be lawful for any court, sheriff, deputy sheriff, coroner or other public officer within this Commonwealth, to demand or receive of the said Lynch, any such tax, levy, charge or contribution.

2. This act shall commence and be in force from and after the passing thereof.

1827. Chapter 130. – An ACT concerning the devisees of William Mount, deceased.

(Passed February 19th, 1827)

WHEREAS, it is represented to the General Assembly by Thomas C. Mount, son and administrator of William Mount, deceased, together with the guardians of the infant children and heirs of the said deceased, that, by the will of the said William Mount, who died in the year eighteen hundred and sixteen, it is directed that all his estate, real and personal, should be kept together undivided, until his youngest child, (now only eleven years old,) shall attain the age of twenty-one years, and then be sold, and the proceeds divided equally among his wife and children: That in consequence of the great diminution in the annual profits of the estate, the same is entirely insufficient for the support and education of the children; and that a constitutional predisposition to consumption, generally manifest among the members of the family, of which disease, the mother and two children have already died, and two others are now without hope of recovery, render it, as is believed, essentially necessary for the preservation of the lives of the survivors, that they should remove to a more southern climate, which they are unable to do without the pecuniary means, to be derived from the sale of the said property; and they have accordingly petitioned that such sale be now authorised by law:

1. BE *it therefore enacted by the General Assembly*, That it shall and may be lawful, for any one or more of the heirs or devisees of the said William Mount, deceased, to file his or their bill either in the Superior Court of Chancery for the district of Fredericksburg, or in any county court within the jurisdiction of which either of the heirs or devisees of the said William Mount, may reside, making the other parties interested in the estate of the said deceased defendants. And the said court is hereby authorised and required to take cognizance of such cause; and if by the answers of the defendants, either in person or by guardian *ad litem*, or by other

evidence, it shall appear to the said court, that a sale and division of the said estate among the several parties entitled to distribution, under the will of the said William Mount, deceased, will promote the interests of the said parties, the same shall be decreed accordingly. And the said court shall make all such orders in the said cause, for the execution of said decree, and the preservation of the rights of the infants, as the said court may deem expedient: *Provided*, That if any of the heirs or devisees of the said William Mount, deceased, shall depart this life previous to the period at which such sale would have been made under the will of the said Mount, deceased, the share of the proceeds of such sale, to which such deceased heir or devisee may be entitled, shall descend as real estate, and not as personalty.

2. This act shall be in force from the passage thereof.

1827. Chapter 131. – An ACT authorising a sale of certain lands whereof James S. Gilliam died seized, and for other purposes.

(Passed March 8th, 1827)

WHEREAS, it appears to the General Assembly, that Doctor James S. Gillam, late of the town of Petersburg, deceased, died seized of several tracts of land in the counties of Dinwiddie and Prince George, and by his last will and testament, which was duly recorded in the hustings court of the town of Petersburg, devised his lands in the county of Dinwiddie, commonly called *Hatcher's run plantation*, (comprehending the lands which he purchased of Skipwith, Fisher, Boisseau and Traylor,) to his son Theophilus F. Gilliam, for life, remainder to his children, and their issue; and failing such issue; with sundry remainders over to the testator's other children, and their issue: and by his said will, he devised, with the like limitations, his plantation in the county of Prince George, commonly called *Blackwater*, to his son Robert Gilliam, as by the said will, recorded as aforesaid, will fully appear: And it being represented, that the said lands are poor, and altogether unprofitable, but being near the town of Petersburg, and well covered with wood, would sell for a good price, and that it would be greatly to the benefit, as well of the said Theophilus F. Gilliam and Robert Gilliam, as of the devisees in remainder, if the said lands were sold, and the money arising from the sales laid out in the purchase of other lands more fertile and advantageous, which cannot be done without the direction of the General Assembly, as the said Theophilus F. Gilliam and Robert Gilliam are only tenants for life: and application being made by them, with the concurrence of the devisees in remainder now living, for the passage of an act for that purpose:

1. *Be it enacted*, That the said lands, lying in the counties of Dinwiddie and Prince George, devised as aforesaid, to the said Theophilus F. Gilliam and Robert Gilliam, shall be, and they are hereby vested in Randolph Harrison, Henry E. Watkins, Edwin Turpin, William R. Johnson, Edward Watkins, Jos'h Goodwin, John Peter, Richard Williams, Peyton Mason and William I. Parsons, and the survivors and survivor of them, and the heirs of such survivor, in trust that they, or any three of them, shall as soon as may be, sell the said lands for the best price to be had, and convey the same to the purchaser or purchasers in fee simple, and lay out the money arising from the sales thereof, in the purchase of other lands, which they shall cause to be conveyed to the said Theophilus F. Gilliam and Robert Gilliam, junior, respectively, to be held by them instead of the lands devised to them as aforesaid, subject to all the limitations, conditions and remainders over, which are declared in

the said will of Doctor James S. Gilliam, deceased, as fully and effectually, in every respect, as if the same were herein repeated, in relation to the lands so to be purchased: *Provided always*, That nothing herein contained shall be construed to affect the right or title of any person or persons, bodies politic or corporate, to the said lands, or any part thereof, other than those claiming under the will of the said James S. Gilliam, deceased.

2. This act shall be in force from the passage thereof.

1827. Chapter 132. – An ACT releasing to the children of George Carson, a tract of land whereof he died seized.

(Passed March 9th, 1827)

1. *Be it enacted by the general assembly*, That all right, title and interest, which hath accrued, or may accrue to the Commonwealth, or to the president and directors of the Literary Fund, in or to a tract of land, lying in the county of Harrison, containing two hundred acres, whereof George Carson died seized, shall be, and the same is hereby released to Caroline M. Carson, Theophilus R. Carson, Augustus E. Carson, Egbert W. Carson, Emily G. Carson, Malvina W. Carson and Alonzo B. Carson, children of the said George Carson, deceased, equally to be divided among them: Saving, however, to all persons, bodies politic and corporate, other than the Commonwealth, and the president and directors of the Literary Fund, any right, title or interest, which they or any of them might or would have had in or to the said land, or any part thereof, if this act had never passed.

2. This act shall be in force from its passage.

1827. Chapter 133. – An ACT releasing to Charles Robertson and others, the Commonwealth's right to certain real estate.

(Passed March 3d, 1827)

WHEREAS, it is represented to the General Assembly, by Charles Robertson, Alexander M. Robertson, David Robertson, George Robertson, junior, Mary Ann Innes, and Jane Medlin, that their uncle, David Robertson, by his will, devised to them four firth parts of one moiety of all his estate, real and personal, and the remaining fifth of the said moiety, to the testator's sister, Mary Robertson, an alien, residing in the Kingdom of Great Britain; that the said Mary is about the age of sixty five years, unmarried, and there exists no probability of her ever coming to this country: And the said Charles, Alexander, David, George, Mary Ann and Jane having petitioned the Legislature to release to them the Commonwealth's right in the real estate of the said David Robertson, deceased, devised as aforesaid to the said Mary Robertson:

1. *Be it enacted,* That all right, title or interest which hath accrued, or may accrue to the Commonwealth, or to the president and directors of the Literary Fund, in or to the one-fifth of one moiety of the real estate of the said David Robertson, deceased, devised as aforesaid, to the said Mary Robertson, by reason of the alienage of the said Mary, be, and the same is hereby released to the said Charles Robertson, Alexander M. Robertson, David Robertson, George Robertson, junior, Mary Ann Innes and Jane Medlin, to be divided among them, in like manner and proportions, as the four-fifths of the said moiety devised to them by the will of the said

deceased: Saving, however, to all persons, bodies politic and corporate, other than the Commonwealth, and the president and directors of the Literary Fund, any right, title or interest which they, or any of them, might or would have had, in or to the estate hereby released, or any part thereof, if this act had never passed.

2. This act shall be in force from its passage.

1828. Chapter 166. – An ACT allowing Alice E. Farley to remove from this State certain slaves held by her for life.

(Passed February 8, 1828)

WHEREAS, it is represented to the General Assembly, by Alice E. Farley, widow of Philip Farley, deceased, that her brother, John W. Calvin, the guardian of her children, has lived for several years in the State of Alabama, where most of the relations of the said Alice and her children now reside, and to which State the said John intends shortly to remove his said wards: These circumstances render it extremely desirable to the said Alice to be enabled to accompany her children from Virginia; but all her property consists of a life estate in a few slaves, which, by the law of this State, will be forfeited if she remove them out of the Commonwealth without the consent of the reversioners, who being infants, however much they may desire it, are incapable of giving that consent:

1. *Be it therefore enacted*, That it shall be lawful for the said Alice to remove hence to the State of Alabama, the slaves now held by her for life, and in which her infant children have the reversionary interest, without incurring thereby any forfeiture or penalty whatever, under the existing laws of this Commonwealth: *Provided*, That the guardian of the said children shall, by deed in writing, to be entered of record in the court of Chesterfield county, consent to such removal.

2. This act shall be in force from its passage.

1829. Chapter 171. – An ACT releasing to Margaret S. Wagener the Commonwealth's right to a certain legacy.

(Passed January 1, 1829)

1. *Be it enacted by the General Assembly*, That all right, title and interest, which by reason of the alienage of David Arragan, a legatee named in the will of Benjamin Harrison, deceased, formerly of the county of Fauquier, hath accrued or may accrue, to the Commonwealth, or to the President and Directors of the Literary Fund, in or to an annuity of ten pounds for life, left by the said will to the said Arragan, shall be, and the same is hereby released to Margaret S. Wagener, the only child of the said Benjamin Harrison; saving, however, to all persons, bodies politic and corporate, other than the Commonwealth, and the President and Directors of the Literary Fund, any right, title, or interest, which they or any of them, might or would have had, in or to the said legacy or any part thereof, if this act had never passed.

2. This act shall be in force from its passage.

1829. Chapter 174. – An ACT divorcing Rebecca Trueman from her husband John Trueman.

(Passed January 2, 1829)

1. *Be it enacted by the General Assembly,* That Rebecca Trueman, of the county of Chesterfield, shall be, and she is hereby forever divorced from her husband John Trueman; and the power and authority of the said John over the person and property of the said Rebecca, and over the person and property of the child of the said Rebecca, shall henceforth cease and determine; *Provided however,* That nothing in this act contained shall be so construed as to prevent the child of the marriage solemnized between the said John and Rebecca, from inheriting and transmitting inheritance, in the same manner as if this act had never passed; nor shall any thing herein contained be so construed as to permit either the said John or Rebecca to marry during the lifetime of the other.

2. This act shall be in force from its passage.

1829. Chapter 170. – An ACT concerning Humphrey Marshall.

(Passed January 16, 1829)

1. *Be it enacted by the General Assembly,* That the Auditor of Public Accounts be, and he is hereby authorised and required to settle with Humphrey Marshall, or his representative, his commutation of full pay for five years, in lieu of half pay for life, as a captain of artillery in the Virginia line on State establishment, during the revolutionary war; and to issue a warrant on the treasury for the amount, in favour of the said Humphrey Marshall, to be paid out of any money therein not otherwise appropriate: *Provided,* That nothing in this act shall be so construed as to authorise any payment of interest on the amount which may be found due for the services of the said Marshall as aforesaid.

2. This act shall be in force from the passage thereof.

1829. Chapter 173. – An ACT divorcing Mary Alvis from her husband Peter M. Alvis.

(Passed February 12, 1829)

1. *Be it enacted by the general assembly,* That the marriage solemnized between Mary Alvis, of the city of Richmond, formerly Mary Walkley, and Peter M. Alvis, shall be, and same is hereby dissolved; and the power and authority of the said Peter over the person and property of the said Mary, shall henceforth cease and determine: *Provided however,* That nothing in this act contained shall be so construed as to authorise either the said Peter M. Alvis or the said Mary Alvis to marry again during the life of the other; and if either the said Peter M. Alvis or Mary Alvis shall so marry again during the life of the other, he or she so offending shall be subject to all the pains and penalties of bigamy, in the same manner as if this act had never passed.

2. This act shall be in force from its passage.

1829. Chapter 172. – An ACT releasing to sundry citizens of Wood county, parts of the land formerly held by John Jones Waldo.
(Passed February 27, 1829)

1. *Be it enacted by the General Assembly of Virginia*, That the title to so much of the land formerly held by John Jones Waldo, now vested in the Commonwealth or President and Directors of the Literary Fund, by inquisition of escheat taken in the county of Wood, on the twenty-ninth day of August, eighteen hundred and twenty-eight, as respects three hundred acres now held by Peter Anderson; two hundred and forty-seven by John Flinn; one hundred by Joseph Dewey; sixty-six and an half by John Boso; one hundred by George White; one hundred and fifty by Thomas Coleman; and fifty by James Smith, to which they each derive title from and under the Commonwealth's patent to Joseph Howard, executor of Thomas Bently, be, and the same is hereby released to them respectively, also the title to so much thereof as respects one hundred and eighty-six acres now held by Benjamin Mitchell, and two hundred claimed by Michael and Henry Sheets, who derive title thereto from and under that of the aforesaid John Jones Waldo, be, and the same is hereby released to them respectively; also the title to two hundred and five acres claimed by Solomon Cross, under a patent to William Weeden, for the same amount, dated the thirteenth day of May, eighteen hundred and eight, be, and the same is hereby released to said Solomon Cross; also the title to so much thereof as respects thirty seven and an half acres held by Jacob Flinn; one hundred and fifty-seven acres of Absalom Bailey; thirty seven and an half of John A. Winsor; one hundred and fifty of Elisha Timms; one hundred acres of Ezekiel M'Farland; fifty acres of Thomizen Elzey Turner; five hundred of James H. Neale and Peter Anderson; two hundred and eighty acres of Noah Ogden; three hundred of John Pennybacker; fifty of Cynthia Bibby and two hundred and fifty of William Sheets and John Gilpin, now in their respective possessions and held under different patents issued subsequently to the title of the aforesaid John Jones Waldo, be, and the same is hereby released to them respectively, saving, however, to all and every person or persons, body or bodies politic or corporate, all the right, title and property of such person or persons, body or bodies politic or corporate, other than the Commonwealth and the President and Directors of the Literary Fund, their several rights and interests in the same manner as if this act had never passed.

2. This act shall commence and be in force from and after the passing thereof.

1829. Chapter 175. – An ACT authorising a sale of the slaves belonging to the estate of Solomon Jacobs, deceased.
(Passed February 25, 1829)

1. *Be it enacted by the general assembly*, That Hetty Jacobs, widow of Solomon Jacobs, late of the city of Richmond, Joseph Marx and Richard Anderson, the first the guardian of his children, and the last the administrator with the will annexed, shall be, and they are hereby authorised and empowered to make sale of the slaves belonging to the estate of the deceased, upon such terms, and in such manner, as they shall deem expedient; and to vest the proceeds arising from the sale, in stock, which stock, and the profits thereof, shall be held in the same right, and

be subject to the same claims and demands, as the slaves, if not sold, would have been.

2. This act shall be in force from its passage.

1829. Chapter 176. – An ACT authorising a sale of the slaves of Thomas G. Pollard, a lunatic.

(Passed February 27, 1829)

1. *Be it enacted by the general assembly*, That George B. Pollard and Ambrose Pollard, committee of the estate of Thomas G. Pollard, a lunatic, now confined in the hospital at Williamsburg, shall be, and they are hereby authorised and empowered to sell at such time, and in such manner, as to them shall seem best, two slaves, belonging to the estate of said lunatic, the next of kin to the said lunatic assenting to such sale, and pay the proceeds arising from such sale into the public treasury, to be applied, if necessary, towards the support and maintenance of the said lunatic; and if, by reason of his restoration, death, or otherwise, the same should not be so applied, then the said money, or so much thereof as may remain unexpended, to be refunded to the said Thomas G. Pollard, or those who may be entitled to the same.

2. This act shall be in force from its passage.

1830. Chapter 145. – An ACT changing the name of William Crittenden Appleby.

(Passed January 7, 1830)

WHEREAS, William Crittenden Appleby, of the county of Culpeper, has petitioned the present General Assembly, that his name may be changed, and that henceforth he may be called and known by the name of William Crittenden: Therefore,

1. *Be it enacted*, That from and after the passing of this act, the said William Crittenden Appleby shall be called and known only by the name of William Crittenden; and by that name, may sue and be sued, implead and be impleaded, in courts of law and equity.

1830. Chapter 147. – An ACT divorcing Elizabeth Lynch from her husband James Lynch.

(Passed January 23, 1830)

1. *Be it enacted by the General Assembly*, That Elizabeth Lynch, of the county of Wythe, shall be, and she is hereby forever divorced from her husband, James Lynch; and the power and authority of the said James over the person and property of the said Elizabeth, and over the person and property of the child of the said Elizabeth, shall henceforth cease and determine; *Provided*, That nothing in this act contained shall be so construed as to prevent the child of the marriage solemnized between the said James and Elizabeth, from inheriting and transmitting inheritance in the same manner as if this act had never passed; *And provided, also*, That nothing herein contained shall be so construed as to authorise either of the said parties to marry during the life of the other.

2. This act shall be in force from its passage.

1830. Chapter 148. – An ACT divorcing William Simpson from his wife Nancy.
(Passed January 25, 1830)

1. *Be it enacted by the General Assembly*, That the marriage solemnized between William Simpson, of the county of Montgomery, and Nancy his wife, formerly Nancy Hornbarger, shall be, and the same is hereby dissolved, and the said William forever divorced from the said Nancy; and that all right, interest or claim of the said Nancy in or to the estate, real or personal, of the said William, or any part thereof, shall cease and determine henceforth and forever: *Provided*, That nothing in this act contained shall be so construed as to permit either the said William or Nancy to marry during the lifetime of the other.

2. This act shall be in force from its passage.

1830. Chapter 146. – An ACT changing the name of David Shepheard to David Patteson.
(Passed February 8, 1830)

1. *Be it enacted by the General Assembly*, That the name of David Shepheard of the county of Buckingham, be, and the same is hereby changed to that of David Patteson, in conformity to a provision of the last will and testament of David R. Patteson, late of the county of Nelson; and that he hereafter be known and called by the name of David Patteson.

2. This act shall be in force from its passage.

1830. Chapter 144. – An ACT concerning George Dodson.
(Passed February 10, 1830)

1. *Be it enacted by the General Assembly*, That George Dodson, of the county of Pittsylvania, a soldier of the revolution, who was wounded in battle, and is now old, poor and infirm, shall be placed on the pension list, and receive sixty dollars annually during his life, and be paid as other pensioners are paid: he shall also receive thirty dollars for his present relief, for which the Auditor of Public Accounts is hereby authorised and required to issue a warrant on the Treasury in favour of the said Dodson, to be paid to him, or to his representatives, out of any money therein not otherwise appropriated.

2. This act shall be in force from its passage.

1830. Chapter 149. – An ACT divorcing Ann Rankin from her husband Abner G. Rankin.
(Passed February 19, 1830)

1. *Be it enacted by the General Assembly*, That the marriage solemnized between Abner G. Rankin and Ann his wife, late Ann Fisher,[5] of the county of Augusta, shall be, and same is hereby dissolved; and the power and authority of the said Abner over the person and property of the said Ann, shall henceforth cease and determine. But nothing herein contained shall be construed to relieve the said Abner

---

[5] Legislative Petition, Augusta Co., #A1242, shows that the petitioner, Ann Fisher, married Rankin in 1826 and separated from him after seven months because of his atrocious conduct. *Bill Drawn.*

from the punishment attached to the crime of bigamy, if he shall marry again during the life of the said Ann.

2. This act shall be in force from its passage.

1831. Chapter CCXXXIII. – An ACT divorcing Felix Ferte from his wife Sarah.
(Passed February 23, 1831)

1. *Be it enacted by the General Assembly*, That the marriage solemnized between Felix Ferte of the county of Norfolk, and Sarah his wife, formerly Sarah Waterman, shall be, and the same is hereby dissolved, and the said Felix forever divorced from the said Sarah; and that all right, interest or claim of the said Sarah in or to the estate, real or personal, of the said Felix, or any part thereof, shall cease and determine henceforth and forever.

2. This act shall be in force from its passage.

1831. Chapter CCXXXII. – An ACT concerning certain devisees of Creed Tanner, deceased.
(Passed March 29, 1831)

WHEREAS, it is represented to the general assembly by Elizabeth Tanner, of the county of Pittsylvania, and Elizabeth C. Oliver, of the county of Halifax, that Creed Tanner, late husband of the said Elizabeth Tanner, being seized in fee of a tract of land, containing one hundred and seventy-three and a half acres, lying on both sides of Birch creek, and adjoining the lands of Lodwich Brown, John Yeaman and others, by his will, duly proved and recorded, devised the same to the said Elizabeth Tanner for life, and after her death to the said Elizabeth C. Oliver, during her natural life, with remainder to the heirs of her body, (except Cynthia L. and Creed Oliver,) in fee: That since the death of the testator it has been ascertained that a gold mine, supposed to be of considerable value exists on the land; and the said Elizabeth Tanner and Elizabeth C. Oliver, being unable to work the same, have contracted with William R. Hagood, Daniel Verser and John H. Tanner, to open and work the mine till the twenty-fifth of December, eighteen hundred and forty-two, who after defraying charges, are to pay one half of the profits to the said Elizabeth Tanner, she binding herself to pay to the said Elizabeth C. Oliver, guardian of her children, the aforesaid devisees in the remainder, who are infants, for their use and benefit, one-fourth of the said profits, that is, a moiety of the monies to be received by the said Elizabeth Tanner; and in case of her death, during the continuance of the contract, the said Elizabeth C. Oliver binding herself to appropriate to the use of her said children, the like portion of the profits which may be received by her under the said contract. But the said William R. Hagood, Daniel Verser and Joel H. Tanner, have hitherto failed to comply with the said contract on their part, alleging that tenants for life have no power to open mines, and consequently they the said Hagood, Verser and Tanner, may be liable to the devisees in remainder for the whole profits. And the said Elizabeth Tanner and Elizabeth C. Oliver, believing the said contract beneficial, as well to the said infants as to themselves, have petitioned the legislature to pass an act ratifying and confirming the same on their behalf:

1. *Be it enacted by the General Assembly*, That if the county court of Pittsylvania shall, upon mature consideration be of opinion that the interests of the

infant devisees aforesaid will be promoted by the execution and performance of the above recited contract, they shall enter such opinion of record; and thereupon, the Said Elizabeth C. Oliver, guardian of the said infants, shall be fully authorized and empowered for them and on their behalf, to sign, seal and acknowledge the said contract; which shall then bind them and control their interests, touching the matters thereof, in the same manner and to the same extent, as if the said devisees, being of full age, had sealed and delivered for themselves. And the said county court, shall if they deem it necessary or proper, either at the time of recording their aforesaid opinion or thereafter, require an additional bond and surety of the said guardian, for the protection and security of the rights of the said infants under the said contract; and in case of her failure to give such additional bond and surety, the said court may remove her, and appoint for them another guardian, who, upon complying with such order as the court may make in the premises, shall have and exercise the powers conferred by this act.

2. This act shall be in force from its passing.

1831. Chapter CCXXXIV. – An ACT divorcing Alexander W. Mills from his wife Elizabeth.
(Passed April 4, 1831)

1. *Be it enacted by the General Assembly*, That the marriage solemnized between Alexander W. Mills, of the county of Lee, and Elizabeth his wife, formerly Elizabeth Brittain, shall be, and the same is hereby dissolved, and the said Alexander forever divorced from the said Elizabeth; and that all right, interest or claim of the said Elizabeth in or to the estate, real or personal of the said Alexander, or any part thereof, shall cease and determine henceforth and forever.

2. This act shall be in force from the passing thereof.

1832. Chapter CCXLVII. – An ACT changing the name of Henry Sprouse to Henry Wood.
(Passed January 14, 1832)

1. *Be it enacted by the General Assembly*, That Henry Sprouse of the county of Albemarle, shall hereafter have, and bear the name of Henry Wood; by which latter name he shall be known and called, as well in courts of justice as without.

2. This act shall be in force from the passing thereof.

1832. Chapter CCXLIV. – An ACT for relief of James C. and Sarah Luck.
(Passed March 3, 1832)

1. *Be it enacted by the General Assembly*, That James C. Luck and Sarah Luck, late Sarah Chiles, of the county of Caroline, shall be, and they are hereby released and discharged from all the pains and penalties, effects and consequences of a judgment of the circuit superior court of law and chancery of the said county, pronounced against them the thirteenth day of September, eighteen hundred and thirty-one, declaring the marriage between the said parties null and void, and ordering their separation from each other as man and wife; and the marriage aforesaid is hereby confirmed: *Provided, however,* That the said James C. Luck shall pay the

costs of the prosecution and judgment aforesaid; and until the same shall be paid, the said judgment as to the said costs shall remain in force as fully as if this act had never been passed.

2. This act shall be in force from the passing thereof.

1832. Chapter CCXLV. – An ACT confirming the marriage of Robert Cropp and his wife Eliza F.
(Passed March 19, 1832)

1. *Be it enacted by the General Assembly*, That Robert Cropp and Eliza F. his wife, of the county of Stafford, shall be, and they are hereby released and discharged from all the pains and penalties incurred by them or either of them, in consequence of their marriage; which marriage is hereby confirmed, and the parties aforesaid, and their issued, declared to be entitled to all the rights, benefits and privileges, belonging to or arising from the said matrimonial connection.

2. This act shall be in force from the passing thereof.

1832. Chapter CCXLVI. – An ACT changing the name of William Griffin Orgain to William Allen.
(Passed March 14, 1832)

Whereas Richard Griffin Orgain of Petersburg,[6] and his infant son William Griffin Orgain, have petitioned the general assembly, that in order to enable the said infant more effectually to secure the benefit of certain real and personal estate, devised to him by William Allen, late of the county of Surry, his name may be changed in conformity with the will of the devisor, from William Griffin Orgain to William Allen.

1. *Be it therefore enacted*, That henceforth the said William Griffin Orgain, shall have and bear the name of William Allen, by which latter name alone he shall be called and known as well in courts of justice, as without.

2. This act shall be in force from the passing thereof.

1832. Chapter CCXLVIII. – An ACT concerning Abraham Depp, a man of colour.
(Passed March 12, 1832)

1. *Be it enacted by the General Assembly*, That Abraham Depp, a man of colour, emancipated by the will of John Depp, late of the county of Powhatan, shall be allowed to reside in the said county, unmolested, for the term of two years, but no longer; and this privilege is granted for the purpose of enabling him to dispose of his property, devised to him by his late master, and to make such other arrangements and preparations as he may deem necessary for his departure from the commonwealth.

2. This act shall be in force from the passing thereof.

---

[6] Legislative Petition, Surry Co., December 4, 1834, shows the name change is required by the will of the son's great-uncle, Col. William Allen of Clermont, before he could claim property left him. *Referred.*

1833. Chapter 241. – An ACT changing the names of Elias, Daniel H. and William Buse Vance, and for other purposes.
(Passed January 15, 1833)

1. *Be it enacted by the general assembly,* That henceforth Elias Vance, Daniel H. Vance, and William Buse Vance, of the county of Tazewell, shall have and bear the names of Elias V. Harman, Daniel H. Harman, and William Buse Harman, respectively; by which latter names alone they shall be called and known, as well in courts of justice as without. And also shall, by the said latter names, be capable of inheriting any estate, real or personal, of Matthias Harman of said county, their reputed father, in the same manner as if they had been respectively born in lawful wedlock.

2. This act shall commence and be in force from the passing thereof.

1833. Chapter 235. – An ACT concerning Alexander West and John Cutright.
(Passed February 9, 1833)

1. *Be it enacted by the General Assembly,* That Alexander West and John Cutright, of the county of Lewis, two old and infirm soldiers of the revolution, be paid out of any money in the treasury, not otherwise appropriated, the sum of one hundred and four dollars each, in discharge of thirteen months service rendered by them during the revolutionary war, in a company of rangers commanded by captain James Boothe, it appearing to the legislature that the said West and Cutright have never received any compensation for said service.

2. This act shall be in force from and after the passage thereof.

1833. Chapter 237. – An ACT divorcing Susan M. Allen from her husband, Julius C. Allen.
(Passed February 21, 1833)

1. *Be it enacted by the General Assembly,* That the marriage solemnized between Susan M. Allen of the city of Williamsburg, formerly Susan M. Eaton, and her husband, Julius C. Allen, shall be, and the same is hereby dissolved, and the said Susan forever divorced from the said Julius; and all power and authority of the said Julius over the person and property of the said Susan, and over the person and property of the child or children of the said Susan, shall cease and determine henceforth and forever.

2. This act shall be in force from the passing thereof.

1833. Chapter 238. – An ACT divorcing Hannah Magee from her husband, Hugh Magee.
(Passed February 28, 1833)

1. *Be it enacted by the general assembly of the commonwealth of Virginia,* That the marriage solemnized between Hugh Magee and Hannah his wife, late Hannah Thornburgh, of the county of Morgan, shall be, and the same is hereby dissolved, and the said Hannah forever divorced from the said Hugh; and that all power and authority of the said Hugh over the person and property of the said Hannah, and over the person or property of any child or children of the said Hannah,

shall cease and determine henceforth and forever. But nothing herein contained shall prevent the child or children born of the said marriage, from inheriting and transmitting inheritance in the same manner as if this act had never been passed.

2. This act shall be in force from the passing thereof.

1833. Chapter 240. – An ACT divorcing Susan W. Bell from her husband, Fielding Bell.

(Passed March 6, 1833)

1. *Be it enacted by the general assembly of the commonwealth of Virginia*, That the marriage between Fielding Bell and Susan W. his wife, who was formerly Susan W. Jarratt, shall be, and the same is hereby dissolved, and the said Susan forever divorced from the said Fielding; and that all right, power and authority of the said Fielding over the person and property of the said Susan W., and over the person and property of any child or children of the said Susan, shall cease and determine henceforth and forever. But nothing in this act contained shall be construed to prevent the children of the said marriage from inheriting and transmitting inheritance in the same manner as if this act had never passed.

2. This act shall be in force from the passing thereof.

1833. Chapter 239. – An ACT divorcing William B. Williams from his wife Mildred.

(Passed March 7, 1833)

1. *Be it enacted by the general assembly of the commonwealth of Virginia*, That the marriage lately solemnized between William B. Williams, of the county of Franklin, and Mildred C. his wife, formerly Mildred C. Tate, shall be, and the same is hereby dissolved, and the said Williams forever divorced from the said Mildred; and that all right, interest or claim of the said Mildred in or to the estate, real or personal, of the said Williams, or any part thereof, shall cease and determine henceforth and forever.

2. This act shall be in force from its passage.

1833. Chapter 242. – An ACT changing the name of James T. Morriss to that of George Whitfield Morriss.

(Passed March 7, 1833)

1. *Be it enacted by the general assembly*, That the name of James T. Morriss, of the county of New Kent, be, and same is hereby changed to that of George Whitfield Morriss, in conformity with a provision in the will of the late doctor George Whitfield Morriss, of the county of New Kent aforesaid, and that hereafter he be known and called by that name.

2. This act shall be in force from its passage.

1833. Chapter 243. – An ACT concerning William Wharton and others.
(Passed March 5, 1833)

Whereas it appears to the general assembly, that William Wharton, Lemuel Wharton, Barney Wharton, Nancy Wharton and Lewis Wharton, of the county of Stafford, who were heretofore held in slavery by John Cooke, senior, deceased, and acquired their freedom since May, eighteen hundred and six, are not negroes or mulattoes, but white persons, although remotely descended from a coloured woman; and they having petitioned the general assembly to be released form the operation of the statute requiring all slaves emancipated since May, eighteen hundred and six, to remove beyond the limits of this commonwealth:

1. *Be it enacted by the general assembly*, That the said William Wharton, Lemuel Wharton, Barney Wharton, Nancy Wharton and Lewis Wharton, shall be, and they are hereby released and discharged from all pains, forfeitures and penalties whatsoever, incurred by them, or any of them, or to which they or any of them may be subject or liable, by reason of their failure heretofore or hereafter to remove beyond the limits of this commonwealth.

2. This act shall be in force from the passing thereof.

1833. Chapter 244. – An ACT allowing certain free persons of colour to remain within this commonwealth for a limited time.
(Passed March 4, 1833)

Whereas it is represented by petition and otherwise, to the general assembly, that by the last will and testament of Abraham Vanmeter, late of the county of Hardy, Charles Bruce, Isaac Bruce, Andrew Bruce, Hannibal Bruce, Rebecca Bruce, and Sarah Bruce their mother, people of colour, and slaves of said Abraham, were emancipated, and property both real and personal, to a considerable amount, devised to them; that the said Sarah, the mother, is very old, in the decline of life, and in the course of nature cannot be expected to linger long; that she is too far advanced in life to encounter a long journey or voyage to another country; that George, Jacob, Solomon, Mary and Mildred (commonly called Milly) Bruce, children also of the said Sarah, are still held in bondage by Elizabeth Vanmeter, widow of the said Abraham, deceased, during her natural life; and asking that those who are now free under the will aforesaid, may remain within this commonwealth, and reside in the county aforesaid, until the death of the said Elizabeth Vanmeter, and one year afterwards; at which time the said mother Sarah, may also be dead, and those who are now slaves will be free, and when all may together leave the commonwealth. And whereas the said Elizabeth Vanmeter has proposed under her hand and seal, to grant, for the use of said emancipated slaves, so much open land as may be necessary, in addition to the wood land and other property devised to them by the will aforesaid, as will prevent either of them becoming chargeable to the county, so soon as they obtain permission to remain as aforesaid; and sundry citizens of said county having testified to said proposal, and certified that said emancipated persons are all civil, harmless and honest: Therefore,

1. *Be it enacted by the general assembly*, That the said Charles Bruce, Isaac Bruce, Andrew Bruce, Hannibal Bruce, Rebecca Bruce, and Sarah Bruce their mother, people of colour, shall be, and they are hereby permitted to remain as free persons within this commonwealth, and to reside in the said county of Hardy, until the

death of Elizabeth Vanmeter, (widow of Abraham Vanmeter late of said county,) and one year afterwards, but no longer. And it is hereby declared, that one reason for granting this privilege is, for the purpose of enabling them to dispose of their property, devised to them by their late master, by affording them time; and to make such other arrangements and preparations, as they (and others concerned in the event of the death of said Elizabeth Vanmeter,) may deem necessary for their departure from this commonwealth: *Provided however*, That if the said Charles, Isaac, Andrew, Hannibal, Rebecca and Sarah Bruce, or either of them, shall hereafter be convicted by the verdict of a jury, and the judgment of a court, of any offence against the laws of this commonwealth, it shall be lawful for the court of the said county of Hardy, or for the court of that county or corporation, within which the conviction and judgment may be had, a majority of the acting justices being present, or having been summoned for that purpose, and the said parties, or either of them, against whom proceedings as aforesaid, shall have been had, having been duly summoned, to shew cause against it, to revoke the leave of residence hereby granted, if deemed expedient, and thereupon to order him or her to depart, forthwith, from this commonwealth. And if, after such order of revocation, he or she shall remain within this commonwealth more than twelve months, he or she shall forfeit his or her right to freedom, and be subject to presentment, prosecution and sale, in the manner provided by the laws of this commonwealth, then in force, concerning slaves, free negroes and mulattoes.

2. This act shall be in force from the passing thereof.

1833. Chapter 268. – An ACT changing the names of Jacqueline P., Martha C., Mary C. and Matilda A. Howle, to that of Jacqueline Lewis Poindexter, Martha C. Poindexter, Mary C. Poindexter and Matilda A. Poindexter.
(Passed December 13, 1833)

1. *Be it enacted by the general assembly*, That henceforth Jacqueline P. Howle, Martha C. Howle, Mary C. Howle and Matilda A. Howle of the county of New Kent, shall have and bear the names of Jacqueline Lewis Poindexter, Martha C. Poindexter, Mary C. Poindexter and Matilda A. Poindexter, respectively, by which latter names alone, they shall be called and known, as well in courts of justice as without, and also shall, by the said latter names, be capable of inheriting any estate, real or personal, in the same manner as if their names had not been changed.

2. This act shall commence and be in force from the passing thereof.

1834. Chapter 266. – An ACT divorcing Joseph Gresham from his wife Sarah W.
(Passed February 15, 1834)

1. *Be it enacted by the general assembly*, That the marriage heretofore solemnized between Joseph Gresham[7] of the county of James City, and Sarah W. his wife, formerly Sarah W. Christian, be, and the same is hereby dissolved, and the said Joseph forever divorced from the said Sarah W.; and that all right, interest or claim of the said Sarah W. in or to the estate, real or personal, of the said Joseph, or any part thereof, by virtue of the said marriage, shall cease and determine henceforth

[7] Legislative Petition, James City Co., December 10, 1833, shows that the Sarah W. Christian was formerly of Charles City Co., and the petitioner sought divorce from her for adultery and having a bastard child by a mulatto man. *Bill Drawn.*

and forever.

2. This act shall be in force from the passing thereof.

1834. Chapter 265. – An ACT concerning David W. Sleeth, and others.

(Passed March 13, 1834)

1. *Be it enacted by the general assembly,* That David W. Sleeth, sold surviving heir of John Sleeth, deceased, who was a sergeant in the company commanded by captain James Booth, in an expedition against the Indians during the revolutionary war, be allowed the sum of one hundred and thirty dollars, for thirteen months services of his said father as sergeant as aforesaid, and Joseph Parsons, John Tucker, James Brown, and Phebe Cunningham, widow of Thomas Cunningham, deceased, shall be allowed the sum of one hundred and four dollars each, for their services as privates, for the same time in the said company; and the auditor of public accounts is hereby authorized and required to issue a warrant on the treasury, in favor of the said Sleeth, Parsons, Tucker, Brown and Cunningham, respectively, for the same, to be paid to them or their representatives out of any money therein not otherwise appropriated.

2. This act shall be in force from its passage.

1834. Chapter 267. – An ACT divorcing William P. Bayliss from his wife Rebecca.

(Passed March 6, 1834)

1. *Be it enacted by the general assembly of Virginia,* That the marriage solemnized between William P. Bayliss of the county of Fairfax, and Rebecca his wife, formerly Rebecca Birch, shall be and the same is hereby dissolved, and the said William forever divorced from the said Rebecca; and that all right, interest and claim of the said Rebecca, in or to the estate, real or personal, of the said William, or any part thereof, shall cease and determine henceforth and forever.

2. This act shall be in force from the passing thereof.

1835. Chapter 213. – An ACT allowing Scipio Lucas and wife to remain in the county of Rockbridge a limited time.

(Passed January 3, 1835)

1. *Be it enacted by the general assembly of Virginia,* That for the purpose of enabling Scipio Lucas, a man of colour, residing in the county of Rockbridge, who has lately been emancipated by the reverend John D. Ewing, to obtain the necessary means in order to the removal of himself and his wife Peggy out of the commonwealth, the said Scipio Lucas and his said wife be, and they are hereby allowed to reside in the said county of Rockbridge, unmolested, for the term of two years, but no longer; and if at any time within that period, the county court of Rockbridge shall see cause to order the said Scipio Lucas and his said wife, or either of them, to depart the commonwealth, they shall have full power so to order, and thenceforth the leave of residence hereby granted shall cease.

2. This act shall be in force from and after the passing thereof.

1835. Chapter 214. – An ACT concerning Margaret, sometimes called Margaret Moss, a free woman of colour.
(Passed January 31, 1835)

Whereas, it appears to the general assembly that Margaret, sometimes called Margaret Moss, who is advanced in life and never had children, has lately been emancipated by Thomas Griffin of the county of York, upon condition that the said Margaret should remain in the service of the family of her late master, until by her annual hire, the consideration of her emancipation should be paid; that the said Margaret is now in the service of the family of the said Griffin, in fulfilment of the condition aforesaid, and that the time of seven years is requisite, at the hire agreed upon, to enable the said Margaret to comply with the conditions upon which her emancipation was granted:

1. *Be it enacted by the general assembly of Virginia*, That the said Margaret, sometimes called Margaret Moss, shall be, and she is hereby permitted to remain as a free person, in the family and service of the said Thomas Griffin, within this commonwealth for the term of seven years, but no longer: *Provided*, That if within the said seven years, the said Margaret shall be convicted by the verdict of a jury, or the judgment of a court of record, of any offence against the laws of this commonwealth, the privilege herein granted shall cease and determine from the time of such conviction.

2. This act shall be in force from and after the passing thereof.

1835. Chapter 210. – An ACT to change the name of Mary Jane Land to Mary Jane Smith.
(Passed February 10, 1835)

1. *Be it enacted by the general assembly*, That henceforth Mary Jane Land of the county of Nansemond shall have and bear the name of Mary Jane Smith, by which latter name alone, she shall be called and known, as well in courts of justice as without, and also shall by the said latter name be capable of inheriting any estate, real or personal, in the same manner as if her name had not been changed.

2. This act shall commence and be in force from the passage thereof.

1835. Chapter 211. – An ACT divorcing Ann Kellum from her husband Benjamin Kellum.
(Passed February 16, 1835)

1. *Be it enacted by the general assembly of Virginia*, That the marriage heretofore solemnized between Ann Kellum, formerly Ann Bray, and Benjamin Kellum, shall be, and the same is hereby dissolved, and said Ann forever divorced from her husband the said Benjamin, and the power and authority of the said Benjamin over the person and property of the said Ann, and over the person and property of the children of the said Ann, shall henceforth cease and determine: *Provided, however*, That nothing herein contained shall be so construed as to prevent the children of the said marriage from inheriting and transmitting inheritance in the same manner as if this act had never passed.

2. This act shall be in force from and after the passing thereof.

1835. Chapter 212. – An ACT divorcing Lucy Watts from her husband James L. Watts.

(Passed February 18, 1835)

1. *Be it enacted by the general assembly of Virginia*, That the marriage heretofore solemnized between Lucy Watts[8] of the county of Amherst, and James L. Watts, shall be, and the same is hereby dissolved, the said Lucy forever divorced from her husband the said James L. Watts, and the power and authority of the said James L. over the person and property of the said Lucy, and over the person and property of the children of the said Lucy by the marriage aforesaid, shall cease and determine: *Provided, however*, That nothing herein contained shall be so construed as to prevent the children of the said marriage from inheriting and transmitting inheritance in the same manner as if this act had never passed.

2. This act shall commence and be in force from and after the passing thereof.

1836. Chapter 263. – An ACT concerning Duff Green.

(Passed February 16, 1836)

WHEREAS it is represented to the general assembly that Duff Green of the town of Falmouth, who commanded a company of riflemen in the forty-fifth regiment of the militia of this commonwealth, received from the commissary general sixty rifles with accoutrements for the purpose of arming and equipping the company commanded by him, and executed his bond, with Thomas Brown his security, on the seventeenth day of February, eighteen hundred and twenty, to Thomas M. Randolph, then governor of this commonwealth, in the penalty of one thousand four hundred dollars, conditioned to keep the said rifles and accoutrements at all times in complete order, and subject to the orders of the executive of Virginia: And whereas by a fire which recently occurred in the said town of Falmouth, the said rifles and accoutrements have been so injured or destroyed as to prevent compliance with the condition of the said bond, and the said Duff Green having petitioned for relief in the premises: Therefore,

1. *Be it enacted by the general assembly*, That the said Duff Green and his said security be, and they are hereby absolved from all liability to the commonwealth by reason of the said bond.

2. This act shall be in force from the passage thereof.

1836. Chapter 267. – An ACT concerning the John Pittenger, late sheriff of Brooke county.

(Passed March 18, 1836)

WHEREAS it appears to the general assembly that the lists of insolvents in the militia fines for the years eighteen hundred and thirty-two and thirty-three, in the county of Brooke, returned by John Pittenger, late sheriff of the said county, have been rejected by the auditor, and payment thereof refused by him, in consequence of the said lists not having been certified within the time and in the manner required

---

[8] Legislative Petition, Amherst Co., #A1014, shows that the divorce was on the grounds of desertion and adultery. Watts left his wife, formed a connection with a free negress, entered the U.S. army and deserted, and is said to have served a term in prison for horse-stealing. *Reported.*

by law. And it also appearing that the certificate required could not be had within the time limited, because of the failure of the officers belonging to the one hundred and third regiment in the county aforesaid, to form a regimental court of enquiry: Therefore,

1. *Be it enacted by the general assembly*, That the auditor of public accounts be, and he is hereby authorized and required to settle with the said John Pittenger the lists of insolvents so by him returned as aforesaid, in the same manner as if they had been certified within the time and in the mode now required by law, crediting the said John Pittenger with the amount thereof at the time they should have been paid into the treasury.

2. This act shall be in force from the passage thereof.

1836. Chapter 271. – An ACT divorcing Ann Edmunds from her husband John W.A. Edmunds.
(Passed March 22, 1836)

1. *Be it enacted by the General Assembly*, That the marriage solemnized between John W.A. Edmunds and Ann Edmunds his wife, formerly Ann Kirk, shall be, and the same is hereby dissolved, and the said Ann forever divorced from the said John W.A. Edmunds; and that the power and authority of the said John W.A. Edmunds over the person and property of the said Ann, shall henceforth entirely cease and determine.

2. This act shall be in force from the passing thereof.

1836. Chapter 272. – An ACT changing the name of William H. Riggan to that of William H. Drewry.
(Passed March 21, 1836)

1. *Be it enacted by the general assembly*, That henceforth William H. Riggan of the county of Surry, shall have and bear the name of William H. Drewry; by which latter name alone, he shall be called and known, as well in courts of justice as without.

2. This act shall be in force from its passage.

1837. Chapter 329. – An ACT authorizing the sale of the land belonging to Joseph Howard, a person of unsound mind, and for other purposes.
(Passed March 30, 1837)

WHEREAS it is represented to the general assembly, that Mary Howard, the wife of Joseph Howard, and William Howard, Richard H. Howard, Jane C. Howard, Ann H. Littlepage, formerly Ann H. Howard, and Douglass Tunis and Maria his wife, formerly Maria Howard, that the said Joseph Howard, who is at this time and has been for the last twenty-five years of insane mind, without any known lucid intervals whatever, is entitled to a tract of land in the county of Powhatan, containing about six hundred or seven hundred acres, and a small personal property; that his children, the said William, Richard H., Jane C., Ann H. and Maria, are all of full age, and together with his wife, the said Mary, are anxious to remove to Missouri or some other western or south-western state, but are detained in their present situation on account of the unfortunate affliction of the said Joseph, of whose recovery no hopes are not entertained, and asking authority to sell the said tract of land, and to invest the proceeds arising therefrom, after deducting so much as may be necessary to remove the said Joseph and family, in such other lands and property as may be most likely to promote the interest of all concerned:

1. *Be it enacted by the general assembly*, That the county court of Powhatan county shall have power and authority upon the application of the parties aforesaid, to authorize the committee of the said Joseph Howard to sell the said tract of land on such terms as the said county court may deem most expedient and beneficial to the parties interested therein; and moreover, direct the proceeds arising from such sale, after deducting the expenses of removing the said Joseph and family, to be invested in such lands and other property as the court may direct: *Provided however*, That at least one moiety of the nett proceeds of the said sale shall be invested in real estate; and that the committee before making sale of the said tract of land, shall enter into bond with sufficient security before the court of the said county, in a penalty equal to double the amount of the land so directed to be sold, conditioned to perform the orders and decrees of the court in relation to the sale and investment of the proceeds aforesaid.

2. *And be it further enacted*, That if the committee of the said Joseph Howard should fail or refuse to give the bond and security herein before required, the said county court of Powhatan shall appoint one or more commissioners to carry into effect such orders and decrees as may be made for the sale of the said land and the investment of the proceeds arising therefrom. The said committee, commissioner or commissioners who may act, shall at the next court to be held for the said county of Powhatan after the sale effected by him or them, of the said tract of land, return to the court of that county a true account thereof, to be by the said court entered of record. And it shall moreover be the duty of the said committee, commissioner or commissioners who may act, within six months after the investment herein authorized is made, to return to the said court a full account of his or their proceedings, which if approved by the court, shall also be entered of record.

3. This act shall be in force from its passage.

1837. Chapter 336. – An ACT divorcing John Barnes from his wife Lilly Barnes.
(Passed March 25, 1837)

1. *Be it enacted by the general assembly*, That the marriage heretofore solemnized between John Barnes and Lilly his wife, formerly Lilly Heldridge, shall be, and the same is hereby dissolved, and the said John forever divorced from his wife, the said Lilly; and that all right, interest and claim of the said Lilly in or to the estate real or personal of the said John, or any part thereof, shall cease and determine henceforth and forever.

2. This act shall be in force from the passing thereof.

1837. Chapter 337. – An ACT divorcing Ann Eliza Eubank from her husband Alfred Eubank.

(Passed March 23, 1837)

1. *Be it enacted by the general assembly*, That the marriage heretofore solemnized between Alfred Eubank and Ann Eliza his wife, of the county of King William, shall be, and the same is hereby dissolved, the said Ann Eliza forever divorced from her husband the said Alfred Eubank, and the power and authority of the said Alfred over the person and property of the said Ann Eliza shall henceforth cease and determine.

2. This act shall be in force from the passing thereof.

1837. Chapter 338. – An ACT divorcing Elizabeth Huston from her husband Robert Huston.

(Passed January 24, 1837)

1. *Be it enacted by the general assembly*, That the marriage heretofore solemnized between Elizabeth Huston, formerly Elizabeth Corbin, and Robert Huston, of the county of Harrison, shall be, and the same is hereby dissolved; the said Elizabeth forever divorced from her husband, the said Robert, and the power and authority of the said Robert over the person and property of the said Elizabeth, and over the persons and property of the children of the said Elizabeth, shall henceforth cease and determine: *Provided however*, That nothing herein contained shall be construed as to prevent the children of the said marriage from inheriting and transmitting inheritance in the same manner as if this act had never passed.

2. This act shall be in force from and after the passing thereof.

1837. Chapter 339. – An ACT divorcing John B. Kirk from his wife Mary Kirk.

(Passed January 24, 1837)

1. *Be it enacted by the general assembly*, That the marriage solemnized between John B. Kirk, of the county of Hardy, and Mary his wife, shall be, and the same is hereby dissolved, and the said John forever divorced from the said Mary; and that all right, interest or claim of the said Mary, in or to the estate, real or personal, of the said John, or any part thereof, shall cease and determine henceforth and forever.

2. This act shall be in force from its passage.

1837. Chapter 340. – An ACT changing the name of Overton T. and Pamelia Lowry, to Overton T. Gardner and Pamelia M. Gardner.

(Passed March 2, 1837)

1. *Be it enacted by the general assembly*, That Overton T. Lowry and Pamelia M. Lowry, children of Aaron Lowry and Mary his wife, of the county of Louisa, shall henceforth have and bear the name of Overton T. Gardner and Pamelia M. Gardner, by which latter name alone they shall be called and known, as well in courts of justice as without.

2. This act shall be in force from the passing thereof.

1837. Chapter 341. – An ACT changing the name of John Page Harrison to that of Henry Harrison.

(Passed March 29, 1837)

1. *Be it enacted by the general assembly*, That henceforth, John Page Harrison, son of Benjamin Harrison, of the county of Charles City, shall have and bear the name of Henry Harrison, by which latter name alone he shall be called and known, as well in courts of justice as without, and also shall, by the said latter name, be capable of inheriting any estate, real or personal, in the same manner as if his name had not been changed.

2. This act shall be in force from the passing thereof.

1838. Chapter 305. – An ACT changing the name of Catharine, Raleigh and Sally M'Craw to that of Thompson.

(Passed January 15, 1838)

1. *Be it enacted by the general assembly*, That henceforth Catharine, Raleigh and Sally M'Craw, illegitimate children of Nancy M'Craw, deceased, of the county of Grayson, shall have and bear the name of Catharine Thompson, Raleigh Thompson and Sally Thompson, by which latter names alone they shall be called and known, as well in courts of justice as without; and shall also by the said latter name be capable of inheriting any estate, real or personal, in the same manner as if their names had not been changed.

2. This act shall be in force from the passing thereof.

1838. Chapter 306. – An ACT changing the names of Virginia Smith and others to that of Armstrong.

(Passed March 7, 1838)

1. *Be it enacted by the general assembly*, That henceforth Virginia Smith, Lewis W. Smith, Mary Anne Smith and Elizabeth Smith, of the county of Louisa, children of Anne Smith and William Armstrong, of the said county, shall have and bear the name of Virginia Armstrong, Lewis W. Armstrong, Mary Anne Armstrong and Elizabeth Armstrong, by which latter name they shall be called and known, as well in courts of justice as without, and also shall, by the said latter name, be capable of inheriting any estate, real or personal, in the same manner as if their names had not been changed.

2. This act shall be in force from passing thereof.

1838. Chapter 299. – An ACT divorcing Elenorah A. Allison from her husband Lemuel R. Allison

(Passed March 23, 1838)

1. *Be it enacted by the general assembly*, That the marriage heretofore solemnized between Lemuel R. Allison and Elenorah A. his wife, formerly Elenorah A. Neff, of the county of Hampshire, shall be, and the same is hereby dissolved; the said Elenorah A. forever divorced from her husband, the said Lemuel R., and the power and authority of the said Lemuel R. over the person and property of the said Elenorah A. and over the persons and property of the children of the said Elenorah

A. shall henceforth cease and determine: *Provided however*, That nothing herein contained shall be construed to prevent the child or children of the said marriage from inheriting and transmitting inheritance in the same manner as if this act had never passed.

2. This act shall be in force from the passing thereof.

1838. Chapter 301. – An ACT divorcing Richard B. Hall from his wife Sarah.
(Passed March 19, 1838)

1. *Be it enacted by the general assembly*, That the marriage heretofore solemnized between Richard B. Hall and his wife Sarah, (formerly Sarah Paul,) of the county of Orange, shall be, and the same is hereby dissolved; the said Richard B. forever divorced from his wife, the said Sarah, and all right, title or interest of the said Sarah in or to the estate, real or personal, of the said Richard B. Hall, shall henceforth cease and determine.

2. This act shall be in force from the passing thereof.

1838. Chapter 302. – An ACT divorcing George Heyden from his wife Mary Anne.
(Passed March 13, 1838)

1. *Be it enacted by the general assembly*, That the marriage heretofore solemnized between George Heyden, of the county of Smyth, and Mary Anne his wife, (formerly Mary Anne Weddell,) shall be, and the same is hereby dissolved, and the said George forever divorced from the said Mary Anne, and that all right, interest or claim of the said Mary Anne in or to the estate, real or personal, of the said George, or any part thereof, shall cease henceforth and forever.

2. This act shall be in force from the passing thereof.

1838. Chapter 304. – An ACT changing the names of Indiana, Mary E., Josiah and John Lightfoot to that of Wilson.
(Passed March 20, 1838)

1. *Be it enacted by the general assembly*, That henceforth Indiana, Mary E., Josiah and John Lightfoot, illegitimate children of [blank] Lightfoot and Josiah Wilson, shall have and bear the names of Indiana Wilson, Mary E. Wilson, Josiah Wilson, and John Wilson, by which latter names they shall be called and known as well in courts of justice as without.

2. This act shall be in force from its passing.

1838. Chapter 303. – An ACT divorcing Elizabeth A. Pannill from her husband Edmund Pannill.
(Passed April 4, 1838)

1. *Be it enacted by the general assembly*, That the marriage heretofore solemnized between Edmund Pannill[9] and Elizabeth A. his wife, of the county of King

---

[9] Legislative Petition, King William Co., March 5, 1837.

William, shall be, and the same is hereby dissolved, and the said Elizabeth A. forever divorced from the said Edmund, and that the power and authority of the said Edmund over the person and property of the said Elizabeth A. shall henceforth cease and determine.

2. This act shall be in force from the passing thereof.

1838. Chapter 300. – An ACT divorcing Sally Ballinger from her husband Richard Ballinger.
(Passed April 6, 1838)

1. *Be it enacted by the general assembly*, That the marriage heretofore solemnized between Richard Ballinger and Sally his wife, formerly Sally Wade,[10] of the county of Bedford, shall be, and the same is hereby dissolved; the said Sally forever divorced from her husband, the said Richard, and the power and authority of the said Richard over the person and property of the said Sally, and over the persons and property of the children of the said marriage, shall henceforth cease and determine: *Provided however*, That nothing herein contained shall be construed to prevent the children of the said marriage from inheriting and transmitting inheritance in the same manner as if this act had never passed.

2. This act shall be in force from the passing thereof.

1839. Chapter 262. – An ACT divorcing Mary Cloud from her husband William Cloud.
(Passed April 6, 1839)

1. *Be it enacted by the general assembly*, That the marriage heretofore solemnized between Mary Cloud and William Cloud, shall be, and the same is hereby dissolved, the said Mary forever divorced from her husband the said William, and the power and authority of the said William over the person and property of the said Mary, shall henceforth cease and determine.

2. This act shall be in force from the passing thereof.

1839. Chapter 263. – An ACT divorcing Jane L. Evans from her husband Ephraim Evans.
(Passed February 13, 1839)

1. *Be it enacted by the general assembly*, That the marriage heretofore solemnized between Ephraim Evans and Jane L., his wife, formerly Jane L. Wardsworth, shall be, and the same is hereby dissolved; the said Jane L. forever divorced from her husband the said Ephraim, and the power and authority of the said Ephraim over the person and property of the said Jane L., and over the persons and property of the children of the said marriage, shall henceforth cease and determine: *Provided, however*, That nothing herein contained shall be construed to prevent the children of the marriage aforesaid from inheriting and transmitting inheritance in the

---

[10] Legislative Petition, Bedford Co., #A1803, petition by Sally Ballinger on grounds of abuse and open adultery. *Referred.*

same manner as if this act had never passed.

2. This act shall be in force from the passing thereof.

1839. Chapter 267. – An ACT allowing to Jefferson Bowen a sum of money.
(Passed March 27, 1839)

1. *Be it enacted by the general assembly*, That the fine of thirty dollars, collected by Jefferson Bowen, deputy sheriff of Cabell county, by virtue of an execution which was issued from the circuit superior court of law and chancery for the county of Cabell, against Sarah Field, for retailing ardent spirits without license, and which was paid by him into the treasury, be and the same is hereby refunded; and the auditor of public accounts is hereby authorized and directed to issue his warrant on the treasury in favour of the said Bowen, to be paid to him or his representative out of any money therein not otherwise appropriated.

2. This act shall be in force from the passing thereof.

1839. Chapter 264. – An ACT divorcing John Grandstaff from his wife Susan.
(Passed April 6, 1839)

1. *Be it enacted by the general assembly*, That the marriage heretofore solemnized between John Grandstaff of the county of Augusta, and Susan his wife, shall be and the same is hereby dissolved, and the said John forever divorced from his wife the said Susan; and that all right, interest and claim of the said Susan in or to the estate, real or personal, of the said John, or any part thereof, shall henceforth cease and determine.

2. This act shall be in force from the passing thereof.

1839. Chapter 265. – An ACT divorcing Elizabeth Watson from her husband Richard P. Watson.
(Passed April 2, 1839)

1. *Be it enacted by the general assembly*, That the marriage heretofore solemnized between Elizabeth Watson of the county of Prince Edward, in this state, and Richard P. Watson, now of the state of Alabama, shall be, and the same is hereby dissolved, and the said Elizabeth forever divorced from her husband the said Richard P. Watson; and the power and authority of the said Richard P. over the person and property of the said Elizabeth, shall henceforth cease and determine.

2. This act shall be in force from the passing thereof.

1839. Chapter 266. – An ACT concerning Mary A. Ball and John S. Hughes.
(Passed April 9, 1839)

1. *Be it enacted by the general assembly*, That the school commissioners of the county of Rappahannock, be and they are hereby authorized and required to pay out of any surplus of the quota of their said county now in their hands to Mary A. Ball the sum of twenty-six dollars and thirty-five cents, and to John S. Hughes the sum of twenty dollars and eighty-four cents, the said sums being the amount due the said

Mary A. Ball and John S. Hughes, respectively, for tuition of poor children in the said county.

2. This act shall be in force from its passage.

1840. Chapter 191. – An ACT releasing to Susan C. Bott the commonwealth's right to a lot in the town of Petersburg for a limited time.
(Passed March 10, 1840)

WHEREAS it is represented by Susan C. Bott, that John Stewart, late of the town of Petersburg, by a nuncupative will a short time before his death, gave his estate to a trustee for the sole use of his illegitimate daughter Mary Anne, then the wife of Andre Thomas Vizzoneau; that the said Stewart was a foreigner and had no relations known to his Petersburg acquaintances; that a part of his estate consisted of the lot upon which he resided, which, not passing under the said will, the legislature in January, eighteen hundred and seventeen, released to the said Mary Anne, during life, the commonwealth's right to the said lot, and then to her issue at her death; that the said Mary Anne conveyed to the said Susan C. Bott one half of the said lot in fee simple, and the other half to Eliza Niblo by deed, in which the same is particularly described, bearing date the fourth day of December, eighteen hundred and twenty-four, and of record in the hustings court of the said town of Petersburg, who have ever since held possession thereof; that after the death of the said Andrew, the said Mary Anne intermarried with another foreigner named Shreve, and has since died without issue, so that the said lot is liable to escheat; and asking the legislature to release to her and the said Eliza Niblo the commonwealth's right thereto: Therefore,

1. *Be it enacted by the general assembly*, That the estate, right, title and claim whatever, which has accrued or may accrue to the commonwealth of Virginia, or to the president and directors of the literary fund, in or to the lot of land hereinbefore described, shall be and the same is hereby released to the said Susan C. Bott for and during her natural life and no longer.

2. This act shall be in force from the passing thereof.

1841. Chapter 161. – An ACT divorcing Jane Smith from her husband Hiram *alias* Highland Smith.
(Passed March 15, 1841)

1. *Be it enacted by the general assembly*, That the marriage heretofore solemnized between Jane Smith, formerly Jane Paulean, and Hiram *alias* Highland Smith, shall be, and the same is hereby dissolved, and the said Jane forever divorced from bed and board, from the said Hiram *alias* Highland; and the power and authority of the said Hiram *alias* Highland over the person and property of the said Jane shall henceforth cease and determine. And the said Jane and her children, begotten during her marriage with William Heath, shall hold and enjoy all property derived to them in consequence of said marriage, by deed, will or otherwise, and be capable in law of receiving and transmitting property, in all respects, in the manner as if the marriage of the petitioner with Hiram Smith had never taken place. But nothing in this act shall be construed so as to permit either of the parties to contract matrimony

72

again, during the lifetime of the other.

    2. This act shall be in force from the passing thereof.

1841. Chapter 71. – An ACT concerning divorces.
(Passed March 17, 1841)

    1. *Be it enacted by the general assembly*, That the circuit superior courts of law and chancery within this commonwealth shall have jurisdiction to hear and determine suits for the dissolution of marriage, where the causes alleged therefor shall be *natural or incurable impotency of body*, at the time of entering into the matrimonial contract, idiocy, bigamy, or for any other cause for which marriage is annulled by the ecclesiastical law; and in such suits, upon full and satisfactory evidence, independently or the confession or admission of either party; the said courts shall have power by definitive sentence, to pronounce and decree the marriage to be null and void; such suits shall be prosecuted according to the rules of proceeding in chancery in said courts, except that the defendant shall not be compelled to answer upon oath, and that the bill shall in no case be taken for confessed, but if the defendant shall fail to answer, the cause shall be set for trial, and the court may proceed to decide it upon the evidence adduced.

    2. *And be it further enacted*, That the said circuit superior courts of law and chancery shall have cognizance of matrimonial causes on account of adultery, cruelty, just cause of bodily fear, abandonment and desertion, or for any other cause for which a limited divorce is authorized by the principles of the ecclesiastical law; and in such cases may grant divorces *a mensa et thoro*, in the usual method of proceeding in said courts, in suits of chancery. In such causes, however, the bill shall in no instance be taken for confessed.

    3. And be it further enacted, That in granting divorces *a mensa et thoro* for causes which justify such divorces by the principles of the ecclesiastical law, the said courts shall have full power to decree perpetual separation, and protection to the persons and property of the parties; to decree to either out of the property of the other, such maintenance as may be proper; to restore to the injured party (as far as practicable) the rights of property conferred by the marriage upon the other; and so to dispose of the custody and guardianship, and provide for the maintenance of the issue of the marriage, as under all the circumstances may seem right. A decree of perpetual separation from the bed and board, shall have the same effect upon the rights of property which either party may acquire after the decree, as a divorce *a vinculo matrimonii* would have, save only, that no such decree of separation from bed and board, shall authorize either party to marry again, during the life of the other; and that another marriage after such a decree, shall expose the offender to the same pains and penalties as if such decree had never been made.

    4. *And be it further enacted*, That the costs in suits for divorce, shall be same as in other suits in chancery, and may be adjudged against either party, according to the discretion of the court.

    5. *And be it further enacted*, That either party may obtain an appeal to the court of appeals from any decree made in any suit under this act, in the same manner as in other suits; and the same time shall be allowed to absent defendants, to set aside any such decree, as is allowed in other cases; and all acts and parts of acts

coming within the purview of this act, shall be, and the same are hereby repealed.

6. This act shall be in force from the passing thereof.

1841. Chapter 221. – An ACT changing the names of George Upshur Nottingham and John Henry Nottingham to that of George Littleton Upshur and John Henry Upshur.
(Passed December 17, 1841)

Where it is represented to the general assembly by George Upshur Nottingham and John Henry Nottingham, of the county of Northampton, that they are desirous of having their names changed to that of George Littleton Upshur and John Henry Upshur, and it appearing to the general assembly that prompt action is necessary, and that there is at present no judge of the circuit in which they reside: Therefore,

1. *Be it enacted by the general assembly*, That henceforth the said George Upshur Nottingham and John Henry Nottingham shall have and bear the names of George Littleton Upshur and John Henry Upshur, by which the latter names shall be called and known, as well in courts of justice as without, and also shall by the said latter names be capable of inheriting any estate, real or personal, in the same manner as if their names had not been changed.

2. This act shall be in force from the passing thereof.

1842. Chapter 223. – An ACT divorcing James M. Martin from his wife Rebecca.
(Passed January 24, 1842)

1. *Be it enacted by the general assembly*, That the marriage heretofore solemnized between James M. Martin and Rebecca his wife, shall be and the same is hereby dissolved, and the said James M. forever divorced from the said Rebecca; and that all right, interest or claim of the said Rebecca in or to the estate, real or personal, of the said James M. Martin, or any part thereof, shall henceforth cease and determine.

2. This act shall be in force from the passing thereof.

1842. Chapter 222. – An ACT concerning Sally Moffett of Rockingham county.
(Passed February 19, 1842)

Whereas it is represented to the general assembly, that Sally Moffett of Rockingham county, a woman of unblemished character, did, in the year eighteen hundred and twenty-five, intermarry with a certain John Moffett, then of said county, who in the year eighteen hundred and twenty-six abandoned her without any just cause, and went to the state of Ohio, where he afterwards departed, and has never returned to this commonwealth, nor been heard of for the last ten years, though diligent enquiry for him as been made: And whereas the said Sally Moffett, notwithstanding the legal presumption of the death of her said husband, is prevented from intermarrying again, from the apprehension that by possibility he may still be living:

1. *Be it therefore enacted*, That on application of the said Sally Moffett to the county court of Rockingham county, she having given previous notice thereof by

74

publication for four weeks in some newspaper published in this commonwealth, the said court is hereby authorized and required, either at a quarterly or monthly term thereof, to cause a jury to be impannelled and sworn for the purpose of ascertaining the facts relative to the abandonment of said Sally Moffett by her said husband, and his continual absence from this commonwealth, without having been heard from; and if it shall appear from the verdict of the jury, upon the facts which they shall find, that the said Sally Moffett is a woman of respectable character, that she was abandoned by her said husband without just cause, and that the legal presumption of his death has arisen and is unrepelled, it shall be lawful for the said court thereupon to render such judgment as will have the effect of authorizing the said Sally Moffett to intermarry again, and of causing such future marriage to be as valid in law, and as effectual, to all intents and purposes, as if she had never been previously married, and to prevent her from being subjected to any injurious consequences whatever, arising out of her first marriage aforesaid.

2. This act shall be in force from the passing thereof.

1843. Chapter 170. – An ACT divorcing Jacob Kerns from his wife Mahala.
(Passed January 25, 1843)

1. *Be it enacted by the general assembly,* That the marriage heretofore solemnized between Jacob Kerns and Mahala his wife, of the county of Marion, shall be and the same is hereby dissolved, and the said Jacob forever divorced from his wife, the said Mahala, and all right, title and interest of the said Mahala, in or to the estate, real or personal, of the said Jacob, shall henceforth cease and determine.

2. This act shall be in force from the passing thereof.

1843. Chapter 168. – An ACT concerning Henry Hayes.
(Passed February 21, 1843)

1. Be it enacted by the general assembly, That the auditor of public accounts be and he is hereby authorized and required to issue a warrant on the treasury, in favour of Henry Hayes of Marion county, for the sum of twenty-seven dollars and fifty cents, a balance due for services rendered by him as a ranger in a company commanded by lieutenant Levy Morgan, from the sixth day of October, seventeen hundred and ninety-three, to the first day of January, seventeen hundred and ninety-five, to be paid to the said Hayes, or his representative, out of any money in the treasury not otherwise appropriated.

2. This act shall be in force from the passing thereof.

1843. Chapter 169. – An ACT divorcing Elizabeth C. Hutchings from her husband David W. Hutchings.
(Passed March 11, 1843)

1. Be it enacted by the general assembly, That the marriage heretofore solemnized between David W. Hutchings and Elizabeth C. his wife, of the county of Rockbridge, shall be and the same is hereby dissolved, and the said Elizabeth C. forever divorced from her husband, the said David W., and the power and authority of the said David W. over the person and property of the said Elizabeth C. shall

henceforth cease and determine.

2. This act shall be in force from the passing thereof.

1843. Chapter 80. – An ACT amending the acts passed the 17th of February 1827, and 17th of March 1840, '41, concerning divorces.
(Passed March 11, 1843)

1. *Be it enacted by the general assembly*, That in all cases of divorces *a mensa et thoro*, heretofore decreed, or hereafter to be decreed, for such causes, for which, by the act passed on the seventeenth day of February eighteen hundred and twenty-seven, entitled "an act to prescribe the method of proceedings in suits and on petitions for divorces," and by the act passed on the seventeenth day of March eighteen hundred and forty-one, entitled "an act concerning divorces," the circuit superior courts of law and chancery, sitting in chancery, are authorized to decree such divorces, a decree of perpetual separation, shall have, and be decreed to have had the same effect upon the rights of property, which either party may acquire after the decree of divorce, and upon the personal rights and legal capacities which either party may enjoy and exercise after such decree, as a divorce *a vinculo matrimonii* would have, save only, that no such decree of separation from bed and board, shall authorize either party to marry again, during the lifetime of the other; and that another marriage after such a decree, shall expose the offender to the same pains and penalties as if such decree had never been made.

2. This act shall be in force from the passing thereof.

1844. Chapter 151. – An ACT divorcing Thomas Prickett from his wife Elizabeth.
(Passed January 16, 1844)

1. *Be it enacted by the general assembly*, That the marriage heretofore solemnized between Thomas Prickett of the county of Tyler, and Elizabeth his wife, shall be and the same is hereby dissolved, and the said Thomas forever divorced from his wife the said Elizabeth; and that all right, interest and claim of the said Elizabeth in and to the estate, real or personal, of the said Thomas, or any part thereof shall henceforth cease and determine.

2. This act shall be force from the passing thereof.

1844. Chapter 152. – An ACT for the relief of George Angus and Henry Angus, persons of color.
(Passed February 15, 1844)

Whereas it is represented to the general assembly by James S. Gee, administrator of Judith Angus deceased, a free woman of color, late of the town of Petersburg, that his intestate by a writing under her hand and seal, bearing date the twenty-first day of June eighteen hundred and thirty-two, purporting to be her last will and testament, but which not being properly attested was never admitted to record, emancipated her son George Angus and her grandson Henry Angus, who are slaves; that there are no creditors of her estate, and it is believed there are none who will ever appear to claim it, and asking that the said George and Henry may be emancipated: Therefore,

1. *Be it enacted*, That the said George Angus and Henry Angus shall be, and they are hereby emancipated and declared free, to the same extent they could or would have been had the writing aforesaid been properly attested and duly admitted to record: *Provided however*, That nothing herein contained shall be so construed as to affect in any manner the rights of creditors of next of kin of the said Judith Angus.

2. This act shall be in force from the passing thereof.

1845. Chapter 160. – An ACT divorcing Jacob Bagent from his wife Eleanor.
(Passed February 21, 1845)

1. *Be it enacted by the general assembly*, That the marriage heretofore solemnized between Jacob Bagent of the county of Loudoun, and Eleanor his wife, be and the same is hereby dissolved, and the said Jacob forever divorced from his wife the said Eleanor, and that all right, interest and claim of the said Eleanor, in and to the estate, real or personal, of the said Jacob, or any part thereof, shall henceforth cease and determine.

2. This act shall be in force from the passing thereof.

1845. Chapter 161. – An ACT divorcing William Bartlam from his wife Temperance.
(Passed February 21, 1845)

1. *Be it enacted by the general assembly*, That the marriage heretofore solemnized between William Bartlam of the county of Chesterfield, and Temperance his wife, shall be and same is hereby dissolved, and the said William forever divorced from his wife the said Temperance; and that all right, title and interest and claim of the said Temperance, in and to the estate, real and personal, of the said William, or any part thereof, shall henceforth cease and determine.

2. This act shall be in force from the passing thereof.

1845. Chapter 162. – An ACT divorcing Amanda Crow from her husband Samuel M. Crow.
(Passed February 13, 1845)

1. *Be it enacted by the general assembly*, That the marriage heretofore solemnized between Amanda Crow, late of Campbell county, but now of Buckingham county, in this state, and Samuel M. Crow, of the same state, shall be and the same is hereby dissolved, and the said Amanda forever divorced from her husband the said Samuel M. Crow; and the power and authority of the said Samuel M. over the person and property of the said Amanda, shall henceforth cease and determine.

2. This act shall be in force from the passing thereof.

1845. Chapter 163. – An ACT divorcing George B. Thurman from his wife Lucy Ann.
(Passed February 21, 1845)

1. *Be it enacted by the general assembly*, That the marriage heretofore solemnized between George B. Thurman, of the county of Campbell, and Lucy Ann

his wife, shall be and the same is hereby dissolved, and the said George B. forever divorced from his wife the said Lucy Ann; and that all right, interest and claim of the said Lucy Ann, in and to the estate, real or personal, of the said George B. or any part thereof, shall henceforth cease and determine.

2. This act shall be in force from the passing thereof.

1845. Chapter 164. – An ACT divorcing Margaret Ann Warden from her husband Malachi Warden.

(Passed February 21, 1845)

1. *Be it enacted by the general assembly*, That the marriage heretofore solemnized between Margaret Ann Warden, of the county of Princess Anne, and Malachi Warden of the same county and state of Virginia, shall be and the same is hereby dissolved, and the said Margaret Ann forever divorced from her husband the said Malachi Warden; and the power and authority of the said Malachi over the person and property of the said Margaret Ann, shall henceforth cease and determine.

2. This act shall be in force from the passing thereof.

1845. Chapter 165. – An ACT divorcing Benjamin Wright and his wife Mariam.

(Passed February 19, 1845)

1. *Be it enacted by the general assembly*, That the marriage heretofore solemnized between Benjamin Wright of the county of Jackson and Mariam his wife, shall be and the same is hereby dissolved, and the said Benjamin forever divorced from his wife the said Mariam, and that all right, interest and claim of the said Mariam in and to the estate, real or personal, of the said Benjamin, or any part thereof, shall henceforth cease and determine.

2. This act shall be in force from the passing thereof.

1845. Chapter 166. – An ACT granting power to the county court of Accomack to decide upon the applications of Peter Snead and Richard Chandler to remain in the commonwealth.

(Passed February 19, 1845)

Whereas the county of Accomack is exempted from the operation of the provisions of the act, entitled "an act amending the laws concerning emancipated slaves, free negroes and mulattoes," passed March the twenty-second, eighteen hundred and thirty-seven: And whereas Peter Snead and Richard Chandler, emancipated slaves residents of said county, have petitioned the general assembly for permission to reside within the commonwealth:

1. *Be it enacted by the general assembly*, That the county court of Accomack, constituted according to the provisions of the first session of the before recited act, shall be and they are hereby authorized, upon the application or applications of the said Peter Snead and Richard Chandler, or either of them, to hear and decide upon the said applications, according to the terms and provisions of the before cited act, as fully and effectually as if the county of Accomack had not been exempted from the operation of the provisions of the before recited act.

2. This act shall be in force from the passing thereof.

1846. Chapter 211. – An ACT concerning Henry Tuggle of the county of Patrick.
(Passed January 15, 1846)

1. *Be it enacted by the general assembly*, That the auditor of public accounts be and is hereby authorized and required to issue his warrant on the treasury, payable out of any money therein not otherwise appropriated, in favour of Henry Tuggle, deputy for Clarke Penn, sheriff of Patrick county, for the sum of forty-three dollars and twenty cents, for expenses incurred by him in the employment of an extra guard to assist him in conveying to the penitentiary (pursuant to the judgment of the circuit superior court of law and chancery for said county, pronounced at its fall term eighteen hundred and forty-five), George Belisle, who had been convicted of a felony in the said court, and ordered to be sent to the penitentiary as aforesaid.

2. This act shall be in force from the passing thereof.

1846. Chapter 212. – An ACT divorcing Thompson Adams from his wife Martha Ann.
(Passed January 16, 1846)

1. *Be it enacted by the general assembly*, That the marriage heretofore solemnized between Thompson Adams of the county of Orange, and Ann his wife, formerly Martha Ann Burruss, shall be and the same is hereby dissolved, and the said Thompson forever divorced from the said Martha Ann, and that all right, interest or claim of the said Martha Ann in or to the estate real or personal of the said Thompson Adams, or any portion thereof, shall henceforth cease and determine.

2. This act shall be in force from the passing thereof.

1846. Chapter 213. – An ACT divorcing Leonard G. Bailey from his wife Hannah S.
(Passed January 22, 1846)

1. *Be it enacted by the general assembly*, That the marriage heretofore solemnized between Leonard G. Bailey and Hannah S. his wife, shall be and the same is hereby dissolved, and the said Leonard G. forever divorced from the said Hannah S., and that all right, interest or claim of the said Hannah in or to the estate real or personal of the said Leonard G. Bailey, or any part thereof, shall henceforth cease and determine.

2. This act shall be in force from the passing thereof.

1846. Chapter 214. – An ACT divorcing John H. Batte from his wife Margaret D.
(Passed January 10, 1846)

1. *Be it enacted by the general assembly*, That the marriage heretofore solemnized between John H. Batte and Margaret D. his wife, shall be and the same is hereby dissolved, and the said John H. forever divorced from the said Margaret D., and that all right, interest or claim of the said Margaret D. in or to the estate real or personal of the said John H. Batte, or any part thereof, shall henceforth cease and determine.

2. This act shall be in force from the passing thereof.

1846. Chapter 215. – An ACT divorcing John J. Campbell from his wife Ann Maria.

(Passed January 16, 1846)

1. *Be it enacted by the general assembly*, That the marriage heretofore solemnized between John J. Campbell of the county of Nelson and Ann Maria his wife, formerly Ann Maria Oliver, be and the same is hereby dissolved, and the said John J. forever divorced from the said Ann Maria, and that all right, interest or claim of the said Ann Maria in or to the estate real or personal of the said John J. Campbell, or any part thereof, shall henceforth cease and determine.

2. The act shall be in force from the passing thereof.

1846. Chapter 216. – An ACT divorcing Peter C. Davis from his wife Sarah E.

(Passed January 19, 1846)

1. *Be it enacted by the general assembly*, That the marriage heretofore solemnized between Peter C. Davis of the county of Buckingham, and Sarah E. his wife, formerly Sarah E. Cox, shall be and the same is hereby dissolved, and the said Peter C. forever divorced from the said Sarah E.; and that all right, interest and claim of the said Sarah E. in or to the estate real or personal of the said Peter C. Davis, or any part thereof, shall henceforth cease and determine.

2. This act shall be in force from the passing thereof.

1846. Chapter 217. – An ACT divorcing David C. Phipps from his wife Dorcas.

(Passed January 19, 1846)

1. *Be it enacted by the general assembly*, That the marriage heretofore solemnized between David C. Phipps of the county of Grayson, and Dorcas his wife, formerly Dorcas Stamper, shall be and the same is hereby dissolved, and the said David C. forever divorced from the said Dorcas; and that all right, interest and claim of the said Dorcas in or to the estate real or personal of the said David C. Phipps, or any part thereof, shall henceforth cease and determine.

2. This act shall be in force from the passing thereof.

1846. Chapter 218. – An ACT divorcing Watkins Harper from his wife Martha.

(Passed January 26, 1846)

1. *Be it enacted by the general assembly*, That the marriage heretofore solemnized between Watkins Harper of the county of Essex, and Martha his wife, formerly Martha Brizendine, shall be and the same is hereby dissolved, and the said Watkins forever divorced from the said Martha; and that all right, interest or claim of the said Martha in or to the estate real or personal of the said Watkins Harper, or any part thereof, shall henceforth cease and determine.

2. This act shall be in force from the passing thereof.

1846. Chapter 219. – An ACT divorcing Sarah C.P. Thomas from her husband Francis Thomas, and changing the name of said Sarah C.P. Thomas to Sarah C.P. M'Dowell.
(Passed January 14, 1846)

1. *Be it enacted by the general assembly*, That the marriage heretofore solemnized between Sarah C.P. Thomas, formerly Sarah C.P. M'Dowell, and Francis Thomas, shall be and the same is hereby dissolved; the said Sarah C.P. forever divorced from her husband the said Francis; and the power and authority of the said Francis over the person and property of the said Sarah C.P. shall henceforth cease and determine; and the said Sarah C.P. Thomas shall henceforth have and bear the name of Sarah C.P. M'Dowell, by which latter name alone she shall be called and known in all respects as if she had never been married.

2. This act shall be in force from the passing thereof.

1847. Chapter 274. – An ACT divorcing Amanda Gosling from her husband Palmer Gosling.
(Passed March 20, 1847)

1. *Be it enacted by the general assembly*, That the marriage heretofore solemnized between Palmer Gosling and Amanda his wife, of the county of Greenbrier, shall be and the same is hereby dissolved, and the said Amanda forever divorced from her husband the said Palmer, and the power and authority of the said Palmer over the person and property of the said Amanda, and over the person and property of the children of the said marriage, shall henceforth cease and determine: *Provided however*, That nothing herein contained shall be construed to prevent the children of the said marriage from inheriting and transmitting inheritance in the same manner as if this act had never passed.

2. This act shall be in force from its passing.

1847. Chapter 275. – An ACT divorcing Helen A.W. Hamilton from her husband Robert S. Hamilton.
(Passed February 24, 1847)

1. *Be it enacted by the general assembly*, That the marriage heretofore solemnized between Robert S. Hamilton and Helen A.W. his wife, formerly Helen A.W. Brooke of the county of Spotsylvania, shall be and the same is hereby dissolved; the said Helen A.W. forever divorced from her husband the said Robert S., and the power and authority of the said Robert S. over the person and property of the said Helen A.W. and over the persons and property of the children of the said Helen A.W., shall henceforth cease and determine: *Provided however*, That nothing herein contained shall be construed to prevent the child or children of the said marriage from inheriting and transmitting inheritance in the same manner as if this act had never passed.

2. This act shall be in force from the passing thereof.

1847. Chapter 276. – An ACT divorcing Catharine Hillary from her husband William Hillary.

(Passed March 16, 1847)

1. *Be it enacted by the general assembly*, That the marriage heretofore solemnized between William Hillary and Catharine his wife, formerly Catharine Withers of the county of Rappahannock, shall be and the same is hereby dissolved, and the said Catharine forever divorced from her husband the said William, and the power and authority of the said William over the person and property of the said Catharine shall henceforth cease and determine.

2. This act shall be in force from the passing thereof.

1847. Chapter 277. – An ACT divorcing Lucinda Hughes from her husband Thomas Hughes.

(Passed March 20, 1847)

1. *Be it enacted by the general assembly*, That the marriage heretofore solemnized between Thomas Hughes and Lucinda his wife of the county of Taylor, (formerly Harrison,) shall be and the same is hereby dissolved, and the said Lucinda forever divorced from her husband the said Thomas Hughes, and the power and authority of the said Thomas over the person and property of the said Lucinda, shall henceforth cease and determine.

2. This act shall be in force from its passing.

1847. Chapter 278. – An ACT divorcing James R. Jones from his wife Elizabeth.

(Passed March 22, 1847)

1. *Be it enacted by the general assembly*, That the marriage heretofore solemnized between James R. Jones and his wife Elizabeth, (formerly Elizabeth Collins,) of the county of Ritchie, shall be and the same is hereby dissolved, and the said James R. forever divorced from his wife the said Elizabeth, and all right, title or interest of the said Elizabeth in or to the estate real or personal, of the said James R. shall henceforth cease and determine.

2. This act shall be in force from its passing.

1847. Chapter 279. – An ACT divorcing Nancy D. Lane from her husband George W. Lane.

(Passed March 20, 1847)

1. *Be it enacted by the general assembly*, That the marriage heretofore solemnized between George W. Lane and Nancy D. his wife, (formerly Nancy D. Hasty,[11]) of the county of Surry, shall be and the same is hereby dissolved, the said Nancy D. forever divorced from her husband, the said George W., and the power and authority of the said George W. over the person and property of the said Nancy D. and over the persons and property of the children of the said marriage shall henceforth cease and determine: *Provided however*, That nothing herein contained shall be construed to prevent the children of the said marriage from inheriting and

---

[11] Legislative Petitions, Surry Co., December 3, 1843. *Rejected.*

transmitting inheritance in the same manner as if this act had never passed.

2. This act shall be in force from the passing thereof.

1847. Chapter 280. – An ACT divorcing Abraham George Leatherman from his wife Mary Ellen.

(Passed January 11, 1847)

1. *Be it enacted by the general assembly*, That the marriage heretofore solemnized between Abraham George Leatherman of the county of Hampshire, and Mary Ellen his wife, shall be and the same is hereby dissolved, and the said Abraham George forever divorced from his wife, the said Mary Ellen, and that all right, title and interest and claim of the said Mary Ellen, in and to the estate, real and personal, of the said Abraham George, or any part thereof, shall henceforth cease and determine.

2. This act shall be in force from the passing thereof.

1847. Chapter 281. – An ACT divorcing William R. and Virginia Myers.

(Passed March 9, 1847)

1. *Be it enacted by the general assembly*, That the marriage heretofore solemnized between William R. Myers of the City of Richmond, and Virginia his wife, (formerly Virginia Pollard,) shall be and the same is hereby dissolved, and the said William R. and the said Virginia forever divorced from each other; and that all the right, interest or claim of said Virginia, in or to the estate, real or personal of the said William R. or any part thereof, shall cease henceforth and forever; and all the right, title, interest, claim and demand of the said William R. in and to the estate, real, personal or mixed of the said Virginia, or any part thereof, shall also cease henceforth and forever.

2. *And be it further enacted*, That henceforth the said Virginia shall be known, taken and accepted by the name of Virginia Pollard.

3. This act shall take effect and be in force from the passing thereof.

1847. Chapter 282. – An ACT divorcing Stephen Odell from his wife Eleanor.

(Passed March 23, 1847)

1. *Be it enacted by the general assembly*, That the marriage heretofore solemnized between Stephen Odell of the county of Pulaski, and Eleanor his wife, shall be and the same is hereby dissolved, and the said Stephen forever divorced from the said Eleanor; and that all right, interest or claim of the said Eleanor in or to the estate, real or personal, or the said Stephen Odell, or any part thereof, shall henceforth cease and determine.

2. This act shall be in force from the passing thereof.

1847. Chapter 283. – An ACT divorcing Mary Margaret Sims from her husband Robert Sims.

(Passed March 22, 1847)

1. *Be it enacted by the general assembly*, That the marriage heretofore solemnized between Robert Sims and his wife Mary Margaret of the county of

Botetourt, shall be and the same is hereby dissolved, the said Mary Margaret forever divorced from her husband the said Robert, and the power and authority of the said Robert over the person and property of the said Mary Margaret, and over the persons and property of the children of the said Mary Margaret, shall henceforth cease and determine: *Provided however,* That nothing herein contained shall be construed to prevent the child or children of the said marriage from inheriting and transmitting inheritance in the same manner as if this act had never passed.

2. This act shall be in force from the passing thereof.

1847. Chapter 284. – An ACT divorcing Amanda Woodyard from her husband John Woodyard.
(Passed March 22, 1847)

1. *Be it enacted by the general assembly,* That the marriage heretofore solemnized between John Woodyard and Amanda his wife, formerly Amanda Johnson, of the county of Harrison, shall be and the same is hereby dissolved, the said Amanda forever divorced from her husband the said John, and the power and authority of the said John over the person and property of the said Amanda, and over the persons and property of the children of the marriage, shall henceforth cease and determine: *Provided however,* That nothing herein contained shall be construed to prevent the children of the said marriage from inheriting and transmitting inheritance in the same manner as if this act had never passed.

2. This act shall be in force from the passing thereof.

1847. Chapter 285. – An ACT divorcing Paulina Pendleton Wright from her husband Shelton Wright.
(Passed March 22, 1847)

1. *Be it enacted by the general assembly,* That the marriage heretofore solemnized between Shelton Wright and Paulina Pendleton his wife, of the county of Nelson, shall be and the same is hereby dissolved; the said Paulina Pendleton forever divorced from her husband the said Shelton, and the power and authority of the said Shelton over the person and property of the children of the said Paulina Pendleton and over the persons and property of the said marriage, shall henceforth cease and determine: *Provided however,* That nothing herein contained shall be construed to prevent the children of the said marriage from inheriting and transmitting inheritance in the same manner as if this act had never passed.

2. This act shall be in force from the passing thereof.

1848. Chapter 122. – An ACT prescribing general regulations to govern applications for divorces *a vinculo matrimonii,* and divorcing Robert Moran from his wife Lydia.
(Passed March 18, 1848)

1. *Be it enacted by the general assembly,* That the marriage heretofore solemnized between Robert Moran and Lydia his wife, (formerly Lydia Poe,) of the county of Marion, shall be and the same is hereby dissolved, and the said Robert forever divorced from his wife the said Lydia; and all right, title or interest of the said

Lydia in or to the estate, real or personal, of the said Robert Moran, shall henceforth cease and determine.

And whereas applications to the legislature for divorces *a vinculo matrimonii* are becoming frequent, and occupy much time in their consideration, and moreover involve investigations more properly judicial in their nature, and ought, so far as this legislature can do it, be referred to the judicial tribunals of the state: Therefore,

2. *Be it enacted by the general assembly,* That the circuit superior courts of law and chancery within this commonwealth, on the chancery side thereof, shall have jurisdiction to hear and determine suits for the dissolution of marriage, where the cause therefore is adultery; and in such suits to decree a divorce from the bonds of matrimony, with liberty to both parties thereafter to marry, or with liberty to the innocent or injured party to marry, and deny it to the guilty party: *Provided however,* That the court of the county, city or town wherein the parties or one of them lives, shall alone have jurisdiction; and when the plaintiff shall have left the county, city or town in which the parties have lived together, the adverse party still living in the same county, the suit shall be instituted and heard in the court held for that county: *And provided furthermore,* That this act shall not extend to the plaintiffs not at the time *bona fide* citizens of the commonwealth, nor to any case or cases if the parties have never lived together as citizens of, and as husband and wife in this state; nor to any cause of adultery which shall have occurred in any other state or county, unless the parties at the time of such cause, or before such cause occurred, lived together as citizens of, and as husband and wife in this state.

3. That such suits shall be prosecuted, and in all respects proceeded in according [sic] to the rules of proceeding in said courts, except that the defendant shall not be compelled to answer upon oath, and that the bill shall in no case be taken for confessed; but if the defendant shall fail to answer, the cause shall be set for trial, and the court may proceed to decide it upon the evidence adduced: *Provided however,* That nothing in this act contained shall be so construed as to give any validity to marriages which are void by law.

4. That in granting divorces under this act, the court shall have full power to decree perpetual protection to the person and property of the parties, and to decree to either, out of the property of the other, such maintenance as may seem proper, to restore to the injured party, as far as practicable, the rights of property conferred by the marriage on the other, and so to dispose of the custody and guardianship, and provide for the maintenance of the issue, as, under all the circumstances, may seem right.

5. That the subject of the costs of suit, and the right of appeal to any party shall be governed by the fifth and sixth sections of the act entitled "an act to prescribe the method of proceeding in suits, and on petitions for divorces," passed February seventeenth, eighteen hundred and twenty-seven: subject, however, to the provisions of all subsequent laws regarding appeals from the circuit superior courts of law and chancery to the court of appeals: *Provided however,* That nothing in this act contained shall authorize any of said courts to decree a divorce *a vinculo matrimonii,* although the fact of adultery be established, if the offence was committed by the procurement, or with the connivance of the complainant; nor if it has been forgiven, (and no repetition of the offence,) and the forgiveness established by express proof, or by the voluntary cohabitation of the parties, with knowledge of the fact; nor where the suit has been brought more than five years after the knowledge of the last act of

adultery; nor where the court shall be satisfied from the evidence in the cause that the complainant has been guilty of adultery during the marriage with the defendant.

6. That to prevent divorces by collusion between the parties, as well under this act as under the act of the seventeenth of February eighteen hundred and twenty-seven, the seventeenth of March eighteen hundred and forty-one, and the eighth of March eighteen hundred and forty-three, it shall be the duty of the attorney for the commonwealth in each of the said courts, in all cases where the defendant is not present, or by attorney, defending the application, to appear for the commonwealth, and in the name of the defendant to defend the same; and if the proceedings be under the fourth section of an act to prescribe the method of proceeding in suits, and on petitions for divorces, passed February seventeenth, eighteen hundred and twenty-seven, and the said attorney shall be of opinion that the finding of the jury is against, or unauthorized by the evidence, he shall move the court to set aside the verdict, and to award a new trial as in other cases.

7. That when the proceeding had be under the fourth section of the act last aforesaid, it shall be required of the complainant to prove before the court and jury that he or she as the case may be, had well and truly discharged his or her conjugal obligations to the defendant. And the court shall certify upon the record that there was, or was not evidence before it satisfying the mind of the court that the offences charged were or were not committed by the procurement, or with the connivance of the complainant, or had or had not been forgiven, and that they occurred within or without the period of five years before the institution of the suit; and that the complainant had, or had not been guilty of the same offence or offences charged against the defendant within five years next before the institution of such suit or proceeding in court.

8. This act shall be in force from the passing thereof.

1848. Chapter 358. – An ACT changing the names of Martha Ann M'Lemore and Cherry Tyas M'Lemore to those of Martha Ann Harris and Cherry Tyas Harris.

(Passed April 4, 1848)

1. *Be it enacted by the general assembly*, That henceforth Martha Ann M'Lemore and Cherry Tyas M'Lemore, children of Lewis Harris of the county of Southampton, shall have and bear the names of Martha Ann Harris and Cherry Tyas Harris, by which latter names alone they shall be called and known as well in courts of justice as without.

2. This act shall be in force from the passing thereof.

1848. Chapter 359. – An ACT changing the name of Henry Kalussowski to that of Henry Korwin.

(Passed January 15, 1848)

1. *Be it enacted by the general assembly*, That henceforth Henry Kalussowski, a native of Poland, but now a naturalized citizen of the United States, and a resident of the county of Cabell in this state, shall have and bear the name of Henry Korwin,

by which latter name alone, he shall be called and known, as well in courts of justice as without.

2. This act shall be in force from the passing thereof.

1848. Chapter 360. – An ACT divorcing Rebecca Allen from her husband Mahlon Allen.

(Passed February 7, 1848)

1. *Be it enacted by the general assembly*, That the marriage heretofore solemnized between Mahlon Allen and Rebecca his wife, of the county of Marshall, shall be and the same is hereby dissolved; the said Rebecca forever divorced from her husband, the said Mahlon, and the power and authority of the said Mahlon over the person and property of the said Rebecca and over the persons and property of the children of the said Rebecca, shall henceforth cease and determine: *Provided however*, That nothing herein contained shall be construed to prevent the child or children of the said marriage from inheriting and transmitting inheritance in the same manner as if this act had never passed.

2. This act shall be in force from the passing thereof.

1848. Chapter 361. – An ACT divorcing Martha A. Allison from her husband James G. Allison.

(Passed March 27, 1848)

1. *Be it enacted by the general assembly*, That the marriage heretofore solemnized between James G. Allison and Martha A.[12] his wife, of the county of Fairfax, shall be and same is hereby dissolved, the said Martha A. forever divorced from her husband the said James G., and the power and authority of the said James G. over the person and property of the said Martha A. shall henceforth cease and determine.

2. This act shall be in force from the passing thereof.

1848. Chapter 362. – An ACT divorcing William H. Blackburn from his wife Sarah.

(Passed February 3, 1848)

1. *Be it enacted by the general assembly*, That the marriage heretofore solemnized between William H. Blackburn and Sarah his wife, (formerly Sarah Chapel,) of the county of Henrico, shall be, and the same is hereby dissolved; and the said William H. forever divorced from his wife, the said Sarah, and all right, title or interest of the said Sarah in or to the estate, real or personal of the said William H. Blackburn, shall henceforth cease and determine.

2. This act shall be in force from the passing thereof.

---

[12] Legislative Petition, Fairfax Co., February 15, 1848, #A197, petitioner represents that some time in the year 1843, being of tender years of the age of seventeen, she was married unto James G. Allison of the said county; husband has since starved her of affection and cruelly treated her; he has repetitively left for weeks without notice, and the petitioner believes his mind is impaired. Deposition of Walter Powell, brother-in-law of James G. Allison. *Referred.*

1848. Chapter 363. – An ACT divorcing Scotty Catharine Brown from her husband Orlando W. Brown.
(Passed April 1, 1848)

1. *Be it enacted by the general assembly*, That the marriage heretofore solemnized between Orlando W. Brown and Scotty Catharine his wife, of the county of Shenandoah, shall be and the same is hereby dissolved; the said Scotty Catharine forever divorced from her husband, the said Orlando W. and the power and authority of the said Orlando W. over the person and property of the said Scotty Catharine shall henceforth cease and determine.

2. This act shall be in force from the passing thereof.

1848. Chapter 364. – An ACT divorcing Ruth Buckingham from her husband Elisha Buckingham.
(Passed January 24, 1848)

1. *Be it enacted by the general assembly*, That the marriage heretofore solemnized between Elisha Buckingham and Ruth his wife, of the county of Fayette, shall be, and the same is hereby dissolved; the said Ruth forever divorced from her husband the said Elisha, and the power and authority of the said Elisha over the person and property of the said Ruth and over the persons and property of the children of the said Ruth shall henceforth cease and determine: *Provided however,* That nothing herein contained shall be construed to prevent the children of the said marriage from inheriting and transmitting inheritance in the same manner as if this act had never passed.

2. This act shall be in force from the passing thereof.

1848. Chapter 365. – An ACT divorcing Bertholomew Cassagrande from his wife Angela.
(Passed March 20, 1848)

1. *Be it enacted by the general assembly*, That the marriage heretofore solemnized between Bertholomew Cassagrande of the City of Richmond and Angela his wife, shall be and the same is hereby dissolved, and the said Bertholomew forever divorced from his wife the said Angela, and all right, title or interest of the said Angela in or to the estate, real or personal of the said Bertholomew Cassagrande shall henceforth cease and determine.

2. This act shall be in force from the passing thereof.

1848. Chapter 366. – An ACT divorcing Elias Davis from his wife Huldah.
(Passed January 24, 1848)

1. *Be it enacted by the general assembly*, That the marriage heretofore solemnized between Elias Davis of the county of Grayson and his wife Huldah, shall be, and the same is hereby dissolved; the said Elias forever divorced from his wife, the said Huldah, and all right, title or interest of the said Huldah in or to the estate, real or personal of the said Elias Davis shall henceforth cease and determine.

2. This act shall be in force from the passing thereof.

1848. Chapter 367. – An ACT divorcing Cutlip Falkler from his wife Francina.
(Passed February 11, 1848)

1. *Be it enacted by the general assembly*, That the marriage heretofore solemnized between Cutlip Falkler and Francina his wife, (formerly Francina Bell,) of the county of Nicholas, shall be and the same is hereby dissolved; and the said Cutlip forever divorced from his wife, the said Francina, and all right, title or interest of the said Francina in or to the estate, real or personal of the said Cutlip Falkler, shall henceforth cease and determine.

2. This act shall be in force from the passing thereof.

1848. Chapter 368. – An ACT divorcing George W. Foster from his wife Margaret M.
(Passed January 24, 1848)

1. *Be it enacted by the general assembly*, That the marriage heretofore solemnized between George W. Foster of the county of Nicholas and Margaret M. his wife, shall be and the same is hereby dissolved; and the said George W. forever divorced from his wife, the said Margaret M., and all right, title or interest of the said Margaret M. in or to the estate, real or personal of the said George W. Foster, shall henceforth cease and determine.

2. This act shall be in force from the passing thereof.

1848. Chapter 369. – An ACT divorcing Maria Howell from her husband John Howell.
(Passed March 27, 1848)

1. *Be it enacted by the general assembly*, That the marriage heretofore solemnized between John Howell and Maria his wife of the county of Rockingham, shall be and the same is hereby dissolved; the said Maria forever divorced from her husband, the said John, and the power and authority of the said John over the person and property of the said Maria, shall henceforth cease and determine.

2. This act shall be in force from the passing thereof.

1848. Chapter 370. – An ACT divorcing Daniel M'Ginty from his wife Louisa.
(Passed January 24, 1848)

1. *Be it enacted by the general assembly*, That the marriage heretofore solemnized between Daniel M'Ginty of the county of Marion and his wife Louisa, (formerly Louisa Roberts,) shall be and the same is hereby dissolved; and the said Daniel forever divorced from his wife, the said Louisa, and all right, title or interest of the said Louisa in or to the estate, real or personal of the said Daniel M'Ginty, shall henceforth cease and determine.

2. This act shall be in force from the passing thereof.

1848. Chapter 371. – An ACT divorcing John Peyton from his wife Delila.
(Passed February 9, 1848)

1. *Be it enacted by the general assembly*, That the marriage heretofore solemnized between John Peyton and his wife Delila, (formerly Delila Sheff,) of the county of Cabell, shall be, and the same is hereby dissolved; the said John forever divorced from his wife the said Delila, and all right, title or interest of the said Delila in or to the estate, real or personal, of the said John Peyton, shall henceforth cease and determine.

2. This act shall be in force from the passing thereof.

1848. Chapter 372. – An ACT divorcing Jacob Plum from his wife Mary Jane.
(Passed January 11, 1848)

1. *Be it enacted by the general assembly*, That the marriage heretofore solemnized between Jacob Plum and Mary Jane his wife, of the county of Preston, shall be, and the same is hereby dissolved; the said Jacob forever divorced from his wife the said Mary Jane, and all right, title or interest of the said Mary Jane in or to the estate, real or personal, of the said Jacob Plum, shall henceforth cease and determine.

2. This act shall be in force from the passing thereof.

1848. Chapter 373. – An ACT divorcing William Yonson from his wife Eliza Jane.
(Passed March 27, 1848)

1. *Be it enacted by the general assembly*, That the marriage heretofore solemnized between William Yonson and his wife Eliza Jane, of the county of Loudoun, shall be and the same is hereby dissolved; and the said William forever divorced from his wife the said Eliza Jane, and all right, title or interest of the said Eliza Jane in or to the estate, real or personal, of the said William Yonson, shall henceforth cease and determine.

2. This act shall be in force from the passing thereof.

1849. Chapter 319. – An ACT divorcing Henry Biddle from his wife Delana.
(Passed February 21, 1849)

1. *Be it enacted by the general assembly*, That the marriage heretofore solemnized between Henry Biddle and his wife Delana, of the county of Tyler, shall be and the same is hereby dissolved, and the said Henry forever divorced from his wife the said Delana, and all right, title or interest of the said Delana, in or to the estate, real or personal, of the said Henry Biddle, shall henceforth cease and determine.

2. This act shall be in force from its passage.

1849. Chapter 320. – An ACT divorcing Cynthia A. Calloway from her husband James G. Calloway.
(Passed February 26, 1849)

1. *Be it enacted by the general assembly*, That the marriage heretofore solemnized between James G. Calloway and Cynthia Ann his wife, of Wayne county, shall be, and the same is hereby dissolved; the said Cynthia Ann forever divorced from her husband the said James G., and the power and authority of the said James G. over the person and property of the said Cynthia Ann, and over the persons and property of the children of the said Cynthia Ann, shall henceforth cease and determine: *Provided however*, That nothing herein contained shall be construed to prevent the children of the said marriage from inheriting and transmitting inheritance in the same manner as if this act had never passed.

2. This act shall be in force from the passing thereof.

1849. Chapter 321. – An ACT divorcing Robert H. Mitchell from his wife Mary A.
(Passed February 23, 1849)

1. *Be it enacted by the general assembly*, That the marriage heretofore solemnized between Robert H. Mitchell and his wife Mary A. of the county of Goochland, shall be and the same is hereby dissolved; the said Robert H. forever divorced from his wife the said Mary A., and all right, title or interest of the said Mary A. in or to the estate, real or personal, of the said Robert H. Mitchell, shall henceforth cease and determine.

2. This act shall be in force from its passage.

1849. Chapter 322. – An ACT divorcing Lucy W. Norman from her husband James B. Norman.
(Passed February 6, 1849)

1. *Be it enacted by the general assembly*, That the marriage heretofore solemnized between James B. Norman and Lucy W. his wife, of the county of Henry, shall be, and the same is hereby dissolved; the said Lucy W. forever divorced from her husband, the said James B., and the power and authority of the said James B. over the person and property of the said Lucy W. shall henceforth cease and determine.

2. This act shall be in force from its passage.

1849. Chapter 323. – An ACT divorcing Sarah Ann Raymond from her husband Henry P. Raymond.
(Passed January 22, 1849)

1. *Be it enacted by the general assembly*, That the marriage heretofore solemnized between Henry P. Raymond and Sarah Ann his wife, formerly Sarah Ann Glenn, of the town of Danville, Pittsylvania county, shall be, and the same is hereby dissolved; the said Sarah Ann forever divorced from her husband, the said Henry P., and the power and authority of the said Henry P. over the person and property of the said Sarah Ann, and over the persons and property of the children of the said Sarah Ann, shall henceforth cease and determine: *Provided however*, That nothing herein

91

contained shall be construed to prevent the children of the said marriage from inheriting and transmitting inheritance in the same manner as if this act had never passed.

2. This act shall be in force from the passing thereof.

1849. Chapter 324. – An ACT divorcing Sarah D. Williams from her husband John W. Williams.

(Passed March 1, 1849)

1. *Be it enacted by the general assembly,* That the marriage heretofore solemnized between John W. Williams and Sarah D., his wife, of the county of King & Queen, shall be and the same is hereby dissolved; and Sarah D. forever divorced from her husband the said John W., and the power and authority of the said John W. over the person and property of the said Sarah D., and over the persons and property of the children of the said marriage, shall henceforth cease and determine: *Provided however,* That nothing herein contained shall be construed to prevent the children of the said marriage from inheriting and transmitting inheritance in the same manner as if this act had never passed: *And provided further,* That the passage of this act shall not in any manner affect any right the said Sarah D. may have under the decree of further proceedings of the circuit superior court of law and chancery of King & Queen county, in a suit in said court instituted by the next friend of the said Sarah D., and still depending therein.

2. This act shall be in force from its passage.

1849. Chapter 318. – An ACT concerning Ulysses Hinchman of the county of Logan.

(Passed January 18, 1849)

WHEREAS Ulysses Hinchman was appointed by an order of the county court of Logan, made at March term, eighteen hundred and forty-five, to celebrate the rites of matrimony in said county, and thereupon took the oath of fidelity to the commonwealth, and gave bond and security as required by the ninth section of the act entitled "an act to reduce into one of the several acts to regulate the solemnization of marriages, prohibiting such as are incestuous, or otherwise unlawful, to prevent forcible and stolen marriages, and for the punishment of the crime of bigamy," passed March first eighteen hundred and nineteen, and received from the said court a testimonial as prescribed by the said section; but a doubt has arisen as to the legality of the said appointment, and the validity of the marriages solemnized by him:

1. *Be it enacted by the general assembly,* That the said Ulysses Hinchman shall be deemed to be duly authorized by the said appointment to celebrate the rites of matrimony within the said county of Logan, and shall be subject in all respects to the provisions of the said act in regard to persons authorized by the county courts to celebrate the rites aforesaid, and that all marriages solemnized by him within the said county since the said appointment shall be deemed to have been solemnized by a person legally authorized to solemnize the same.

2. This act shall be in force from the passing thereof.

1849. Chapter 325. – An ACT changing the names of Fleming and Friendless Blood to that of Meredith.
(Passed March 17, 1849)

1. *Be it enacted by the general assembly*, That henceforth Fleming and Friendless Blood, children of Moody Blood, of the county of King William, shall have and bear the name of Fleming Meredith and Friendless Meredith, by which latter names alone they shall be called and known, as well in courts of justice as without, and shall also by the said latter name be capable of inheriting any estate, real or personal, in the same manner as if their names had not been changed.

2. This act shall be in force from the passing thereof.

1849. Chapter 326. – An ACT directing the governor to present a sword to Francis Otway Byrd.
(Passed January 10, 1849)

1. *Be it enacted by the general assembly*, That the governor of the commonwealth be directed to have prepared and to present a sword, with a suitable inscription, to Francis Otway Byrd, a native of Clarke county, Virginia, for his patriotic and gallant conduct and services during the war of eighteen hundred and twelve.

2. This act shall be in force from its passage.

1850. Chapter 319. – An ACT concerning John Tatsapaugh of the town of Alexandria.
(Passed March 14, 1850)

1. *Be it enacted by the general assembly*, That the auditor of public accounts be and he is hereby authorized and directed to issue his warrant upon the treasury, (payable out of any money therein not otherwise appropriated,) in favor of John Tatsapaugh of the town of Alexandria, or his legal representatives, for the sum of forty-two dollars and thirteen cents, the amount of an account for clothing and goods furnished to a company of volunteers raised by Captain Henry Fairfax during the war with Mexico, after the enrolment of the men and before they were mustered into service.

2. This act shall be in force from its passage.

1850. Chapter 324. – An ACT divorcing Amelia H. Beard from her husband John H. Beard.
(Passed March 12, 1850)

1. *Be it enacted by the general assembly*, That the marriage heretofore solemnized between John H. Beard and Amelia H. his wife, of the county of Jefferson, shall be and the same is hereby dissolved; the said Amelia H. forever divorced from her husband the said John H., and the power and authority of the said John H. over the person and property of the said Amelia H., and over the persons and property of the children of the said Amelia H., shall henceforth cease and determine: *Provided however*, That nothing herein contained shall be construed to prevent the children of the said marriage from inheriting and transmitting inheritance

in the same manner as if this act had never passed.

2. This act shall be in force from its passage.

1850. Chapter 325. – An ACT concerning Margaret Fleece of the county of Morgan.

(Passed March 12, 1850)

WHEREAS it is represented to the general assembly that Margaret Alderton of the county of Morgan, on or about the thirty-first of March eighteen hundred and forty-seven, intermarried with one John E. Fleece, then of said county; that she is a woman of irreproachable character; that said marriage was contracted with the consent and approbation of her parents and friends, and that at the date thereof she was only about nineteen years of age; that up to the time of the marriage, the said John E. Fleece was a man of unexceptionable character, but that soon thereafter, to wit, on or about the sixth day of April eighteen hundred and forty-seven, he was arrested on a charge of forgery and committed to the jail of his county, but escaped therefrom before the day fixed for his trial by an examining court, since which time he has neither returned nor been apprehended; and the said Margaret Fleece has petitioned the general assembly for a divorce, *a vinculo matrimonii*: Therefore,

1. *Be it enacted by the general assembly*, That authority is hereby given to the said Margaret Fleece, either in person or by her next friend, to file her bill for a divorce against the said John E. Fleece, in the circuit superior court of law and chancery for the county of Morgan. The said bill shall allege the facts aforesaid, and shall be verified by the oath of the plaintiff or her next friend, and process to answer the same shall be executed by personal service of a copy thereof upon the defendant, if in the commonwealth, or upon affidavit made before the clerk of the court aforesaid by the plaintiff or her next friend, that after diligent enquiry the defendant is believed to be out of the commonwealth, an order of publication may be awarded and executed as in other cases of non-resident defendants, except that the order of publication shall state the object of the bill and the allegations upon which the same is founded. After the cause shall have been matured and set for hearing, the court aforesaid shall direct an issue to be made up and a jury to be empaneled at its bar to try the truth of the allegations hereinbefore recited. If upon the trial of such issue the same be found for the plaintiff, the court aforesaid is hereby authorized and required to enter up its decree in the cause, pronouncing the marriage heretofore solemnized between the said John E. and Margaret Fleece null and void; and thereupon the said Margaret shall take the name of Margaret Alderton, and by such name shall enjoy the rights of a *feme sole* as fully as though she had never been married.

2. In the suit aforesaid the bill shall not be taken for confessed, and whether the defendant answer or not, the cause shall be heard and tried upon legal evidence, independently of the statements or admissions of either party in the pleadings or otherwise, and costs may be awarded as the court shall think proper.

3. This act shall be in force from the passing thereof.

1850. Chapter 326. – An ACT divorcing Martha Goddard from her husband Jared N. Goddard, and David Keblinger from his wife Elizabeth.

(Passed March 20, 1850)

1. *Be it enacted by the general assembly*, That the marriage heretofore solemnized between Jared N. Goddard and Martha his wife, of the county of Marshall, shall be and the same is hereby dissolved; the said Martha forever divorced from her husband the said Jared N., and the power and authority of the said Jared N. over the person and property of the said Martha, and over the persons and property of the children of the said Martha, shall henceforth cease and determine: *Provided however*, That nothing herein contained shall be construed to prevent the children of the said marriage from inheriting and transmitting inheritance in the same manner as if this act had never passed.

2. *And be it further enacted*, That the marriage heretofore solemnized between David Keblinger[13] and his wife Elizabeth, of the county of Albemarle, shall be and the same is hereby dissolved, and the said David Keblinger forever divorced from his wife the said Elizabeth; and all right, title or interest of the said Elizabeth in or to the estate, real or personal, of the said David Keblinger shall henceforth cease and determine.

3. This act shall be in force from the passing thereof.

1850. Chapter 327. – An ACT divorcing Huldah Heiskell from her husband Ferdinand S. Heiskell.

(Passed March 12, 1850)

1. *Be it enacted by the general assembly*, That the marriage heretofore solemnized between Huldah Heiskell,[14] late of Augusta county but now of Rockingham county in this state, and Ferdinand S. Heiskell of the same state, shall be and same is hereby dissolved, and the said Huldah forever divorced from her husband the said Ferdinand S. Heiskell; and the power and authority of the said Ferdinand S. over the person and property of the said Huldah shall henceforth cease and determine.

2. This act shall be in force from the passing thereof.

---

[13] Legislative Petition, Albemarle Co., #A399. Divorce from his wife, formerly Mrs. Elizabeth McCord. She has totally deserted the petitioner and he wishes to secure his property for his children by a former marriage. *Referred.*

[14] Legislative Petition, Augusta Co., #A1373. Divorce from his wife, Huldah, nee Graham, who has herself secured a divorce *a mensa et thoro*. Petitioner married when a very young man; he admits that he got drunk and was sometimes unkind, but maintains that he loved his wife. She left him, owing to her mother's solicitations. Petitioner reformed, joined Methodist Church and led exemplary life; his wife returned to him. He again fell into habit of intoxication and his wife left him again, securing a divorce and $60 a year alimony. Petitioner commuted the alimony for $700, one-third of his property. He now asks for grant of absolute divorce. *Referred.* #A1378, December 11, 1849. Divorce from her husband, Ferdinand S. Heiskell. Augusta Co. Circuit Court has granted petitioner a divorce *a mensa et thoro*.

1850. Chapter 328. – An ACT divorcing Alfred Jacobs from his wife Margaret Ann.
(Passed January 23, 1850)

1. *Be it enacted by the general assembly*, That the marriage heretofore solemnized between Alfred Jacobs and his wife Margaret Ann, of the county of Alexandria, shall be, and the same is hereby dissolved, the said Alfred forever divorced from his wife the said Margaret Ann; and all right, title or interest of the said Margaret Ann in or to the estate, real or personal, of the said Alfred Jacobs, shall henceforth cease and determine.

2. This act shall be in force from its passage.

1850. Chapter 329. – An ACT divorcing Manuel Lewis from his wife Ann.
(Passed March 22, 1850)

1. *Be it enacted by the general assembly*, That the marriage heretofore solemnized between Manuel Lewis and his wife Ann, of the county of Henrico, shall be and the same is hereby dissolved, the said Manuel forever divorced from his wife the said Ann; and all right, title or interest of the said Ann in or to the estate, real or personal, of the said Manuel Lewis, shall henceforth cease and determine.

2. This act shall be in force from its passage.

1850. Chapter 330. – An ACT divorcing Henry C. Moore from his wife Elizabeth.
(Passed March 16, 1850)

1. *Be it enacted by the general assembly*, That the marriage heretofore solemnized between Henry C. Moore and his wife Elizabeth, (formerly Elizabeth Metcalf,) of the county of Randolph, shall be and the same is hereby dissolved, the said Henry C. forever divorced from his wife the said Elizabeth; and all right, title or interest of the said Elizabeth in or to the estate, real or personal, of the said Henry C. Moore, shall henceforth cease and determine.

2. This act shall be in force from the passing thereof.

1850. Chapter 331. – An ACT divorcing Henry Newby from his wife Frances W.
(Passed March 15, 1850)

1. *Be it enacted by the general assembly*, That the marriage heretofore solemnized between Henry Newby of the county of Mecklenburg, and his wife Frances W., shall be and the same is hereby dissolved, the said Henry forever divorced from his wife, the said Frances W.; and all right, title or interest of the said Frances W. in or to the estate, real or personal, of the said Henry Newby shall henceforth cease and determine.

2. This act shall be in force from the passing thereof.

1850. Chapter 332. – An ACT divorcing Elizabeth Ownby from her husband Edward Ownby.

(Passed January 22, 1850)

1. *Be it enacted by the general assembly*, That the marriage heretofore solemnized between Edward Ownby and Elizabeth his wife, of the county of Bedford, shall be and same is hereby dissolved, the said Elizabeth forever divorced from her husband the said Edward; and the power and authority of the said Edward over the person and property of the said Elizabeth, and over the persons and property of the children of the said Elizabeth shall henceforth cease and determine: *Provided however*, That nothing herein contained shall be construed to prevent the children of the said marriage from inheriting and transmitting inheritance in the same manner as if this act had never passed.

2. This act shall be in force from its passage.

1850. Chapter 333. – An ACT divorcing Susan Rollins from her husband Henry Rollins.

(Passed February 9, 1850)

1. *Be it enacted by the general assembly*, That the marriage heretofore solemnized between Henry Rollins and Susan his wife, of the county of Spotsylvania, shall be and the same is hereby dissolved, the said Susan forever divorced from her husband the said Henry, and the power and authority of the said Henry over the person and property of the said Susan, and over the persons and property of the children of the said Susan, shall henceforth cease and determine: *Provided however*, That nothing herein contained shall be construed to prevent the children of the said marriage from inheriting and transmitting inheritance in the same manner as if this act had never passed.

2. This act shall be in force from the passing thereof.

1850. Chapter 334. – An ACT divorcing William Rucker from his wife Elizabeth.

(Passed March 22, 1850)

1. *Be it enacted by the general assembly*, That the marriage heretofore solemnized between William Rucker and his wife Elizabeth, of the county of Alleghany, shall be and the same is hereby dissolved, and the said William forever divorced from his wife the said Elizabeth; and all right, title or interest of the said Elizabeth in or to the estate, real or personal, of the said William Rucker, shall henceforth cease and determine.

2. This act shall be in force from its passage.

1850. Chapter 335. – An ACT divorcing William B. Spencer from his wife Elizabeth.

(Passed March 12, 1850)

1. *Be it enacted by the general assembly*, That the marriage heretofore solemnized between William B. Spencer and his wife Elizabeth, of the county of Scott, shall be and the same is hereby dissolved, the said William B. forever divorced from his wife the said Elizabeth; and all right, title or interest of the said Elizabeth in

or to the estate, real or personal, of the said William B. Spencer, shall henceforth cease and determine.

2. This act shall be in force from its passage.

1850. Chapter 336. – An ACT divorcing James M. Stephens from his wife Mary Ann.

(Passed March 16, 1850)

1. *Be it enacted by the general assembly*, That the marriage heretofore solemnized between James M. Stephens and his wife Mary Ann, of the county of Marshall, shall be and the same is hereby dissolved, the said James M. forever divorced from his wife the said Mary Ann; and all right, title or interest of the said Mary Ann in or to the estate, real or personal, of the said James M. Stephens, shall henceforth cease and determine.

2. This act shall be in force from the passing thereof.

1850. Chapter 334. – An ACT divorcing Mary J. Terry from her husband William B. Terry.

(Passed March 22, 1850)

1. *Be it enacted by the general assembly*, That the marriage heretofore solemnized between William B. Terry and Mary J. his wife, of the county of Goochland, shall be and the same is hereby dissolved, the said Mary J. forever divorced from her husband the said William B., and the power and authority of the said William B. over the person and property of the said Mary J., and over the persons and property of the children of the said Mary J., shall henceforth cease and determine: *Provided however*, That nothing herein contained shall be construed to prevent the children of the said marriage from inheriting and transmitting inheritance in the same manner as if this act had never passed.

2. This act shall be in force from the passing thereof.

1851. Chapter 295. – An ACT changing the name of John James Wells to that of Lackland, and for other purposes.

(Passed March 15, 1851)

B E *it enacted by the General Assembly*, That henceforth John James Wells of the county of Buckingham shall have and bear the name of John James Lackland, by which latter name he shall be called and known, as well in courts of justice as without, and also shall, by the said latter name, be capable of inheriting any estate, real or personal, in the same manner as if his name had not been changed.

2. *Be if further enacted*, That henceforth William W. Finney of the county of Accomack shall have and bear the name of John Arlington, by which latter name alone he shall be called and known, as well in courts of justice as without, and shall also by the said latter name be capable of inheriting any estate, real or personal, in the same manner as if his name had not been changed.

3. This act shall be in force from its passage.

1851. Chapter 296. – An ACT divorcing Eliza Jane Baare from her husband Ferdinand R. Baare.

(Passed January 20, 1851)

B E *it enacted by the General Assembly,* That the marriage heretofore solemnized between Ferdinand R. Baare and Eliza Jane his wife, (formerly Eliza Jane Fisher,) of the town of Alexandria, shall be and the same is hereby dissolved; the said Eliza Jane forever divorced from her husband the said Ferdinand R., and the power and authority of the said Ferdinand R. over the person and property of the said Eliza Jane shall henceforth cease and determine. But the said Ferdinand R. Baare, being the delinquent party, shall not have power again to marry within this state.

2. This act shall be in force from its passage.

1851. Chapter 297. – An ACT divorcing Caroline Octavia Balls of the county of Loudoun, from her husband Robert M. Balls.

(Passed February 27, 1851)

B E *it enacted by the General Assembly,* That the marriage heretofore solemnized between Robert M. Balls and Caroline Octavia his wife, (formerly Caroline Octavia Hodgson,) shall be and the same is hereby dissolved; the said Caroline Octavia forever divorced from her husband the said Robert M., and the power and authority of the said Robert M. over the person and property of the said Caroline Octavia shall henceforth cease and determine.

2. This act shall be in force from its passage.

1851. Chapter 298. – An ACT divorcing Ann Rebecca Beazley from her husband Isaac M. Beazley.

(Passed March 27, 1851)

B E *it enacted by the General Assembly,* That the marriage heretofore solemnized between Isaac M. Beazley and his wife Ann Rebecca, of the county of Page, shall be and the same is hereby dissolved; and the said Ann Rebecca forever divorced from her husband the said Isaac M., and all right, title and interest in and to the estate of the said Ann Rebecca, and the power and authority of the said Isaac M. over the person and property of the said Ann Rebecca, and over the person and persons of the children of the said Ann Rebecca, shall henceforth cease and determine: *Provided however,* That nothing herein contained shall be construed to prevent the children of the said marriage from inheriting and transmitting inheritance in the same manner as if this act had never passed.

2. This act shall be in force from its passage.

1851. Chapter 299. – An ACT divorcing Ann T. Blankinship from her husband Thomas R. Blankinship.

(Passed March 27, 1851)

B E *it enacted by the General Assembly,* That the marriage heretofore solemnized between Thomas R. Blankinship and Ann T. his wife, (formerly Ann T. Potter,) of the county of Patrick, shall be and the same is hereby dissolved; the said Ann T. forever divorced from her husband the said Thomas R., and the power and authority of the said Thomas R. over the person and property of the said Ann T., and over the person and property of the child of the said marriage, shall henceforth cease and determine: *Provided however*, That nothing herein contained shall be construed to prevent the child of the said marriage from inheriting and transmitting inheritance in the same manner as if this act had never passed.

2. This act shall be in force from the passing thereof.

1851. Chapter 300. – An ACT divorcing Margaret A. Combs from her husband Benjamin Combs.
(Passed January 14, 1851)

B E *it enacted by the General Assembly*, That the marriage heretofore solemnized between Benjamin Combs and Margaret A. his wife, (formerly Margaret Edrington,) of the county of Stafford, shall be and the same is hereby dissolved, the said Margaret A. forever divorced from her husband the said Benjamin, and the power and authority of the said Benjamin over the person and property of the said Margaret A. shall henceforth cease and determine.

2. This act shall be in force from its passage.

1851. Chapter 301. – An ACT divorcing Mary Ann Conway from her husband Andrew J. Conway.
(Passed January 9, 1851)

B E *it enacted by the General Assembly*, That the marriage heretofore solemnized between Andrew J. Conway and Mary Ann his wife, of the town of Alexandria, shall be and same is hereby dissolved; the said Mary Ann forever divorced from her husband the said Andrew J., and the power and authority of the said Andrew J. over the person and property of the said Mary Ann, and over the person and property of the child or children of the said marriage, shall henceforth cease and determine: *Provided however*, That nothing herein contained shall be construed to prevent the children of the said marriage from inheriting and transmitting inheritance in the same manner as if this act had never passed.

2. This act shall be in force from its passage.

1851. Chapter 302. – An ACT divorcing Mary E.S. Harris from her husband George W. Harris, and for other purposes.
(Passed March 29, 1851)

B E *it enacted by the General Assembly*, That the marriage heretofore solemnized between George W. Harris and Mary E.S. his wife, of the city of Richmond, shall be and same is hereby dissolved; the said Mary E.S. forever divorced from her husband the said George W., and the power and authority of the said George W. over the person and property of the said Mary E.S., and over the persons and property of the child or children of the said marriage, shall henceforth cease and determine: *Provided however*, That nothing herein contained shall be contained to prevent the child or children of the said marriage from inheriting and transmitting inheritance in the same manner as if this act had never passed.

2. *Be it further enacted*, That henceforth the said Mary E.S. shall be known

and accepted by the name of Mary E.S. Wingfield.

3. *Be if further enacted*, That it shall be lawful for Robert E. Drinkwater of the county of Nottoway to contract and enter into marriage during the lifetime of Henrietta Drinkwater his former wife, from whom he was divorced *a vinculo matrimonii* by the decree of the circuit court of Nottoway county.

4. This act shall be in force from the passing thereof.

1851. Chapter 303. – An ACT divorcing George Johnston from his wife Susannah.
(Passed March 27, 1851)

B E *it enacted by the General Assembly*, That the marriage heretofore solemnized between George Johnston and his wife Susannah, of the county of Wyoming, shall be and the same is hereby dissolved; the said George forever divorced from his wife the said Susannah, and all the right, title or interest of the said Susannah in or to the estate, real or personal, of the said George Johnston, shall henceforth cease and determine.

2. This act shall be in force from its passage.

1851. Chapter 304. – An ACT divorcing John C. Johnson from his wife Elizabeth, and Mary A. Hilliard from her husband Benjamin.
(Passed March 27, 1851)

B E *it enacted by the General Assembly*, That the marriage heretofore solemnized between John C. Johnson and Elizabeth his wife, (formerly Elizabeth Haney,) of the city of Richmond, shall be and the same is hereby dissolved; the said John C. forever divorced from his wife the said Elizabeth, and all right, title or interest of the said Elizabeth in or to the estate, real or personal, of the said John C. Johnson shall henceforth cease and determine.

2. *Be it enacted by the General Assembly*, That the marriage heretofore solemnized between Benjamin Hilliard and Mary A. his wife, (formerly Mary A. Lydick,) of the town of Lynchburg, shall be and the same is hereby dissolved; the said Mary A. forever divorced from her husband the said Benjamin, and the power and authority of the said Benjamin over the person and property of the said Mary A. shall henceforth cease and determine.

3. This act shall be in force from its passage.

1851. Chapter 305. – An ACT divorcing Malinda S. Jones from her husband George Jones.
(Passed March 17, 1851)

B E *it enacted by the General Assembly*, That the marriage heretofore solemnized between George Jones and Malinda S. his wife, formerly Malinda S. Topping, of the city of New York, shall be and the same is hereby dissolved; the said Malinda S. forever divorced from her husband the said George, and the power and authority of the said George over the person and property of the said Malinda S. and over the persons and property of the children of the said marriage shall henceforth cease and determine: *Provided however*, That nothing herein contained shall be construed to prevent the children of the said marriage from inheriting and transmitting inheritance in the same manner as if this act had never passed.

2. This act shall be in force from its passage.

1851. Chapter 306. – An ACT divorcing Joseph S. Polling from his wife Elizabeth.
(Passed March 27, 1851)

B E it enacted by the General Assembly, That the marriage heretofore solemnized between Joseph S. Polling and his wife Elizabeth, (formerly Elizabeth Cool,) of the county of Hampshire, shall be and the same is hereby dissolved; the said Joseph S. Polling forever divorced from his wife the said Elizabeth, and all right, title and interest of the said Elizabeth, in or to the estate, real and personal, of the said Joseph S. Polling, shall henceforth cease and determine.

2. This act shall be in force from the passing thereof.

1851. Chapter 307. – An ACT divorcing Mary A.E. Roberts from her husband Nathaniel G. Roberts.
(Passed January 16, 1851)

B E it enacted by the General Assembly, That the marriage heretofore solemnized between Nathaniel G. Roberts and Mary A.E. his wife, of the city of Norfolk, shall be and the same is hereby dissolved; the said Mary A.E. forever divorced from her husband the said Nathaniel G., and the power and authority of the said Nathaniel G. over the person and property of the said Mary A.E. shall henceforth cease and determine.

2. This act shall be in force from Its passage.

1851. Chapter 308. – An ACT divorcing Henry L. Stephens from his wife Rebecca Jane.
(Passed March 27, 1851)

B E it enacted by the General Assembly, That the marriage heretofore solemnized between Henry L. Stephens and his wife Rebecca Jane, (formerly Rebecca Jane Fleet,) of the county of Clarke, shall be and the same is hereby dissolved; the said Henry L. Stephens forever divorced from his wife the said Rebecca Jane, and all right, title or interest of the said Rebecca Jane, in or to the estate, real or personal, of the said Henry L. Stephens, shall henceforth cease and determine.

2. This act shall be in force from the passing thereof.

1851. Chapter 309. – An ACT divorcing Sarah F. Wilson from her husband John Wilson, and Balthazar Sperat Du Veyriere from his wife Jane R.
(Passed March 27, 1851)

B E it enacted by the General Assembly, That the marriage heretofore solemnized between John Wilson and Sarah F. his wife, of the county of Greenbrier, shall be and the same is hereby dissolved; the said Sarah F. forever divorced from her husband the said John Wilson, and the power and authority of the said John over the person and property of the said Sarah F. shall henceforth cease and determine.

2. *Be it enacted by the General Assembly*, That the marriage heretofore solemnized between Balthazar Sperat Du Veyriere and Jane R. his wife, of Norfolk county, shall be and same is hereby dissolved, and the said Jane R. forever divorced from her husband, the said Balthazar, and the right, power and authority of the said Balthazar to and over the person and property of the said Jane R., and over the persons and property of the children of the said Jane R., shall henceforth cease and determine: *Provided however*, That nothing herein contained shall be construed to prevent the children of the said marriage from inheriting and transmitting inheritance in the same manner as if this act had never passed, except that neither the said Balthazar nor any claiming under him shall be entitled to any estate that may be inherited by or come in possession of the said children from their mother or maternal kindred, either in the direct or collateral line or otherwise.

3. This act shall be in force from its passage.

1851. Chapter 310. – An ACT divorcing Anna Woolfolk from her husband Bentley B. Woolfolk.

(Passed March 22, 1851)

BE *it enacted by the General Assembly*, That the marriage heretofore solemnized between Bentley B. Woolfolk and his wife Anna, (formerly Anna Roane,) of the county of Hanover, shall be and same is hereby dissolved; the said Anna forever divorced from her husband the said Bentley B., and the power and authority of the said Bentley B. over the person and property of the said Anna shall henceforth cease and determine.

2. This act shall be in force from its passage.

1852. Chapter 411. – An ACT to amend the second section of an act, entitled "an act releasing to the heirs of Peter Lower and John Welman the commonwealth's right to certain lands therein mentioned," passed January 11th 1851.

(Passed February 10, 1852)

BE *it enacted by the General Assembly*, That the second section of the act, entitled "an act releasing to the heirs of Peter Lower and John Welman the commonwealth's right to certain lands therein mentioned," passed January eleventh, eighteen hundred and fifty-one, be so amended as to read as follows: That all the estate, right, title, interest and claim whatever, which have accrued to the commonwealth of Virginia, or to the president and directors of the Literary fund, in or to two tracts of land lying and being in the county of Wayne, conveyed by William Thompson to John Welman, by deeds bearing date the sixth day of November eighteen hundred and forty-seven, and the seventeenth day of January eighteen hundred and thirty three, the former of record in the county of Wayne, and the latter of record in the clerk's office of the county of Cabell, shall be and the same is hereby released, transferred and vested in the said John Welman, his heirs and assigns; saving, however, to all bodies politic and corporate other than the commonwealth, any right, title, interest, claim or estate which they or any of them might or would have had in or to the said tracts of land hereinbefore mentioned, in the same manner as if this act had never passed.

    2. This act shall be in force from its passage.

1852. Chapter 412. – An ACT releasing to the widow and daughters of George Raincock the right of the commonwealth to a house and lot in the suburbs of Norfolk, of which John Lawrence died possessed in 1814.

(Passed March 31, 1842)

WHEREAS it is represented to the General Assembly that John Lawrence, a native of England, who resided in Norfolk for some time before the Revolutionary war until his death in eighteen hundred and fourteen, was never married, and died intestate, without any known kindred; that after his death, his countryman and friend George Raincock administered upon his estate and took possession of the house and lot in the suburbs of Norfolk, in which Mr. Lawrence had lived; that Mr. Raincock from that time dwelt thereon, and paid taxes on the same; and that after improving the house, he died about two years ago, leaving the house and lot in the possession of his widow, Rebecca Raincock; and she has petitioned that whatever right the state has in the said house and lot may be released to her and her daughters: Now, therefore,

    1. *Be it enacted by the General Assembly*, That all the right and interest of the commonwealth and of the board of the Literary fund in and to the said house and lot shall be and the same are hereby released unto the said Rebecca Raincock for life, and after her death, unto her daughters. But this release is in nowise to impair or affect any claim, which if this act were not passed, could lawfully be made to the said John Lawrence; nor to impair or affect any other claim thereto than the claim of the commonwealth and the board of the Literary fund.

    2. This act shall be in force from its passage.

1852. Chapter 413. – An ACT releasing to John Robinson and the heirs of Washington Robinson the commonwealth's right to a tract of land therein mentioned.

(Passed February 28, 1852)

BE *it enacted by the General Assembly*, That all right, title and interest which the commonwealth has in and to a tract of land lying and being in the county of Taylor, and containing four hundred acres, returned delinquent for the nonpayment of taxes, in the name of William Hopkins, from the year eighteen hundred and forty-one to the year eighteen hundred and forty-nine, both inclusive, and purchased by the commonwealth, be and the same is hereby released to John Robinson and the heirs of Washington Robinson; the said tract of land having been improperly sold for the nonpayment of taxes.

    2. This act shall be in force from its passage.

1852. Chapter 414. – An ACT releasing to William Yeaton the right of the commonwealth to a lot of land in the town of Alexandria.
(Passed May 3, 1852)

BE *it enacted by the General Assembly,* That all the estate, right, title and claim whatsoever, which has accrued or may accrue to the commonwealth of Virginia, or to the president and directors of the Literary fund, in and to a lot of ground on the north side of [Prince] street, east side of Pitt street, and west side of Royal street, in the town of Alexandria, recently escheated as the property of Edward Herris, shall be and is hereby released to William Yeaton, his heirs and assigns; saving, however, to all persons and bodies politic and corporate, other than the commonwealth, and the president and directors of the Literary fund, any right, title, interest, claim or estate which they or any of them might or would have had in and to the said lot of land, in the same manner as if this act had never passed.

2. This act shall be in force from its passage.

1852. Chapter 424. – An ACT for the relief of Joshua C. Gunnell of the county of Fairfax.
(Passed April 6, 1852)

1. *Be it enacted by the general assembly,* That the auditor of public accounts be and he is hereby authorized and required to issue his warrant on the treasury, payable out of any money therein not otherwise appropriated, in favor of Joshua C. Gunnell, or his legal representatives, for the sum of thirty-one dollars, for supplies furnished by said Gunnell to a company of volunteers for the Mexican war, commanded by the late Captain Henry Fairfax.

2. This act shall be in force from its passage.

1852. Chapter 428. – An ACT for the relief of William H. Muir of the town of Alexandria.
(Passed March 4, 1852)

1. *Be it enacted by the general assembly,* That the auditor of public accounts be and he is hereby authorized and required to issue his warrant on the treasury, payable out of any money therein not otherwise appropriated, in favor of William H. Muir, or his legal representative, for the sum of fifty-three dollars and twenty cents, for supplies furnished by said William H. Muir to a company of volunteers for the Mexican war, commanded by the late Captain Henry Fairfax.

2. This act shall be in force from its passage.

1853. Chapter 556. – An ACT to authorize the clerk of the county court of Fairfax to remove beyond the limits of the commonwealth the original will of George Washington.
(Passed March 22, 1853)

1. *Be it enacted by the general assembly,* That Alfred Moss, the clerk of the county court of Fairfax, be and he is hereby authorized, under the direction and with the permission of the county court of Fairfax, to withdraw from the records of the county court of Fairfax the original will of General George Washington, and to carry

the same beyond the limits of the commonwealth, and to entrust the same to the custody of an engraver, to be selected by him for the purpose of having the said original will lithographed: *provided however*, that the said Alfred Moss shall, before removing the said will, satisfy the county court of Fairfax that he has taken the necessary steps to insure the safe-keeping of the said will while in the hands of the engraver, and to cause the same to be restored to the files of the court, after the same be lithographed.

2. This act shall be in force from and after its passage.

1853. Chapter 556. – An ACT allowing the original will of Edward H. Ker to be temporarily removed from the county court of Accomack.

(Passed April 8, 1853)

1. *Be it enacted by the general assembly*, That the clerk of the county court of Accomack be and he is hereby authorized, under the direction and with the permission of the county court of Accomack, to withdraw from the records of the county court of the said county the original will of Edward H. Ker, and to entrust the same to the custody of the personal representative or representatives of Edward S. Snead, in order that the same may be duly admitted to probate in the county of Somerset in the state of Maryland: provided however, that the said personal representative or representatives shall, before removing the said original will, satisfy the said court, by entering into bond in a sufficient penalty, with satisfactory security, to be approved by said court, conditioned to cause the said original will to be restored to the files of the county court of Accomack after the same shall have been admitted to probate in the said county of Somerset.

2. This act shall be in force from and after its passage.

A PARTIAL LIST OF LEGISLATIVE PETITIONS
INVOLVING DIVORCE

1790, November 16. David Arell. Alexandria, Box B, #A482.

David Arell states he was married in Alexandria in this state in the year [blank] to Phebe Caverley[15] the daughter of Joseph Caverley of that Town who [has] after the marriage discovered signs of infidelity, that in the course of the five years in which he has inhabited with her he has been frequently under the necessity of parting with her in consequence of her adulterous and infamous practices, and that at length she became to base a prostitute that he found it absolutely impossible to live with her any longer... Signed by D. Arell. *Rejected, then Reported.*

1795, November 14. Jacob Egborn. Prince William County, #A3360-a.

Divorce from his wife Delilah Williams to whom he was married in 1786; three years afterwards she eloped without cause. Two months ago he found her living in the town of Dumfries in a state of unrestrained lewdness. William Barnes, justice, witness, claims Dilly Egborn is reputed to be a common prostitute. *Reasonable.*

1796, November 22. Robert Reagh. Bath County, #A1543.

Divorce from his wife, Martha Meek, on rounds of adultery and desertion.

1797, December 13. Margaret [Haggerty] Brown. Augusta County Petitions, #A1175.

Divorce from her husband, John Brown. He has deserted her and besides she heard from good authority that Brown has another wife. *Referred.*

1807, December 23. William Howard. Amherst County Petitions, #A953.

Divorce from his wife, neé Betsy Dean, on the grounds of adultery and desertion. *Reported.*

1809, November 14. William Howard. Amherst County Petitions, #A959.

Divorce from his wife, neé Elizabeth Dean. Wife is an adulteress, having intercourse with both whites and blacks. Petitioner and his wife have separated, and she is willing to be divorced. *Reported.*

1809, December 12. Judith [Hill] Lyon. Amherst County Petitions, #A962.

Divorce from her husband, Alexander Lyon who has pilfered the estate left the petitioner by her father William Hill.

1809, December 12. Sally [Apperson] Dumas. New Kent County Petitions.

Divorce from her husband Benjamin Dumas who has deserted. Husband has taken away with him one of the couple's two children (who has since died) and has reputedly married twice thereafter. *Rejected.*

---

[15] The *Virginia Journal and Alexandria Advertiser*, 12 MAY 1785, p. 3, announced the recent marriage. Alexandria Hustings Court Deeds, Bk. G, p. 312, and the *Alexandria Gazette*, of 1 MAR 1796, p. 3, show that Mrs. Phoebe Arell was married 29 FEB 1796, to Capt. Stephen Moore.

1810, December 17. Sophia McCaughen. Prince William County, #A5700.
Divorce from husband Charles McCaughen, to whom she was married in 1803 while he was a resident of Dumfries. Based on neglect, idleness, and poverty. *Rejected.*

1814, November 2. Richard Jones. Northampton County Petitions.
Divorce from his wife Peggy, who has mothered a mulatto bastard child. *Bill Drawn.*

1814, December 12. Ellen [Shields] Dunlap. Augusta County Petitions, #A1204.
Divorce from her husband, Robert Dunlap, because of ill treatment and his intercourse with a negro woman named Milly, belonging to the petitioner. Dunlap claims this woman and negro boy as coming to him through marriage with the petitioner. *Rejected.*

1815, December 6. Ann Pope. Amelia County Petitions, #A774.
Divorce from her husband, Jacquelin A. Pope. On the grounds of cruelty and desertion. *Bill Drawn.*

1815, December 9. Sophia McCaughen. Prince William County.
Divorce from her husband, Charles McCaughen, to whom she was married July 28, 1803, as Sophia Cave, formerly of the town of Dumfries. Husband became addicted to intemperate habits; he left her and went to Fredericksburg; routinely neglected her and reduced her to poverty. *Referred* and *Rejected, as a house bill was drawn and reported.*

1815, December 12. Edward Morris. Bath County Petitions, #A1565.
Divorce from his wife, Rhoda Morris, on the grounds of adultery. Major Moses Mann named as co-respondent. Depositions and other papers. *Rejected.*

1817, December 11. Elizabeth A. [Finney] Lewis. Accomack County Petitions, #A57.
Divorce from her husband, Stephen J. Lewis. He is probably a British spy, and is a bigamist and swindler. Petitioner's property was attached to pay his debts, but chancery court of Accomack intervened and suspended execution. *Bill Drawn.*

1818, January 2. Margaret Johnston. Augusta County Petitions, #A1222.
Divorce from her husband, Absolem Johnston. He deserted the petitioner and her four children eight years ago and has not been heard from since; he has furthermore married another woman in Tennessee. Property of the petitioner is not safe from Johnston, who may return at any time and seize it. Petitioner does not wish to marry again, as that is felony. *Bill Drawn.*

1818, December 9. Thomas Gill. Nansemond County Petitions.
Petitioner requests to be exempt from penalties of marrying a dead wife's sister under the act in 1818. He married Sarah Paddleford in 1816, at the age of 54, with a proper license with officiating clergyman. *Reasonable.*

108

1818, December 23. Jane D. Godwin. Isle of Wight County Petitions.
Divorce from her husband Edmond Godwin, who battered her in violent rages. He has driven her from her home, and has denied her access to her children who are dying. *Bill Drawn.*

1820, December 11. Delilah Brewer. Fairfax County.
Divorce from her husband John H. Brewer. Petitioner fears husband will submit petition for divorce after learning of her desire for the same; presents her facts. Petitioner found her husband attached to a woman of color, and has been accused by him of having committed adultery.

1822, December 19. Susannah Shultz. Augusta County Petitions, #A1231.
Divorce from her husband, George Shultz. He deserted her and her three children in 1809, and it is believed he has married again. *Rejected.*

1824, December 6. Elizabeth Mills. Albemarle County Petitions, #A256.
Divorce from her husband Martin S. Mills, whom she married when very young. He took her from place to place and failed to supply the necessaries of life. He was finally imprisoned for horse stealing and she returned home. *Reasonable.*

1826, December 8. David Parker. Nansemond County Petitions.
Divorce from his second wife, Jane Miller, who committed adultery with slaves and persons of colour, and who had one or more children of colour. Petitioner's first wife, Jane Carter, died in 1816, leaving him with surviving children. His second wife finally left him and went to North Carolina. *Bill Drawn.*

1826, December 16. Hannah H. Beeton. Augusta County Petitions, #A1243.
Divorce from her husband, Robert Beeton. He is drunken, beats the petitioner, turns her out of house and otherwise ill-treats her. He has sold everything to obtain drink, and finally in 1817 turned petitioner and infant daughter out of doors and began a connection with a woman of ill-fame. Petitioner by hard work has supported herself and child and acquired some household articles, which are liable to be taken at any moment by her husband. *Bill Drawn.*

1828, December 23. Richard Turnell. Accomack County Petitions, #A74.
Divorce from his wife Rosa Turnell, who eloped with another man. *Rejected.*

1831, December 8. William P. Baylis. Fairfax County.
Divorce from wife Rebecca Birch, to whom he was married on April 12, 1827. In three weeks after marriage, wife eloped from petitioner's bed and has never since returned. She has since lived in an open and adulterous situation with a free man of color, named Welford Mortimore, with whom she has since had a bastard child. *Rejected* and *Bill Drawn.*

1834, December 3. Louisa W. Drake. New Kent County Petitions.
Petitioner seeks divorce from husband Robert Drake whose cruelty drove her and the two children out of the house. *Referred.*

1834, December 27. Addison Nottingham. Northampton County Petitions.
Petitioner seeks a divorce from his wife Peggy for her desertion eight years since; believes she has in the meantime married someone else. *Rejected.*

1836, December 9. Ann [Taylor] Eubank. King William County Petitions.
Petitioner seeks divorce from husband Alfred Eubank.

1839, December 4. Asahel Joyner. Southampton County Petitions.
Divorce from his wife Julia Ann Reese because of her repeated adultery with John Ragley. Includes copy of county court case wherein Mr. Joyner began divorce proceedings. *Bill Ordered.*

1839, December 16. Henry D. Warwick. Amherst County Petitions, #A1028.
Divorce from his wife, neé Ann Eliza Ross. He married her in 1838 and just five months and twelve days later she gave birth to a child, of which she confessed her brother is the father. Affidavits of Dr. Robert S. Payne and Dr. William I. Holcombe accompanying. *Rejected.*

1840, January 14. Elizabeth Ann Binns. Amelia County Petitions, #A807.
Divorce from her husband Edmund Binns. Superior court of Amelia has decided for the petitioner on the facts. Court record shows brutality as the cause for divorce suit. *Rejected.*

1840, January 24. Mary Eanes. Amelia County Petitions, #A808.
Divorce from her husband, George H. Eanes. Petitioner has obtained verdict of superior court. Copy of court record showing cause of divorce to be criminal character of Eanes, who is a thief and forger. *Referred.*

1840, February 6. Mary Jones. Alleghany County Petitions, #A673.
Divorce from her husband, Israel Jones. He is drunken, inhuman and in the habit of slandering the petitioner. He deserted her sometime ago but she fears that he will return and assert his marital claims. *Rejected.*

1840, December 2. James Harris. Bedford County, #A1812.
Divorce of his daughter, Martha C. Harris, from her husband, John Hemmings. Hemmings is a thief and swindler and has fled to avoid prosecution. Includes court record. *Bill Drawn.*

1840, December 14. Bryant Rawls. Nansemond County Petitions.
Divorce from his wife Rachel Lester, whom he married in 1827, and who left him and afterward gave birth to a coloured child. *Bill Drawn.*

1840, December 22. Elizabeth B. White. Isle of Wight County Petitions.
Divorce from Husband John L. White, who became an alcoholic and left her in 1834. She has not heard from him since and has raised three daughters. *Rejected.*

1841, January 11. Olimpia [Meredith] Blood. King William County Petitions.
Divorce from her husband Moody Blood.

1843, December 3. Nancy D. [Hasty] Lane. Surry County Petitions.
Divorce from her husband, George W. Lane, who in 1841 murdered her brother Robert Hasty and was sentenced to 18 years in prison. *Rejected, then Bill Drawn.*

1843, December 4. Frances Webb. Albemarle County Petitions, #A245.
Divorce from her husband, Benajah A. Webb, who had run deep into debt from dissipation and then disappeared. It was reported that he had married another woman, and yet Frances Webb's property, left her by her father, is being sold by the sheriff to pay Webb's debts. *Ordered to lie on the table.*

1848, January 8. Sarah Pierce Turner. Nansemond County Petitions.
Divorce from her husband Kinchen Turner, and admits she committed adultery. *Referred.*

1848, January 18. Kinchen Turner. Nansemond County Petitions.
Divorce from his wife, Sarah Pierce, to whom he was married in 1834. They had five children, and afterward he found her with and shot one William R. Butler. *Referred.*

1848, December 18. William F. Hill. Amherst County Petitions, #A1039.
Divorce from his wife, neé Cordelia Thurman, who deserted him three years since. He fears she is living a dissolute life. *Referred.*

1849, December 7. Alfred Jacobs. Alexandria County Petitions, #A582.
Alfred Jacobs petitions the General Assembly for a divorce *à vinculo matrimonii*[16] from his wife, Margaret Ann Jacobs.[17] The petitioner respectfully shows that he desires the General Assembly to grant him an absolute divorce *à vinculo matrimonii* from his said wife, Margaret Ann Jacobs, and that, the grounds his application for such divorce, upon the causes set forth in a statement contained in the record from the clerk's office of the Circuit Superior Court of law & chancery for Alexandria County, Virginia, herewith inclosed. Dated 5 DEC 1849. Signed, Alfred [his mark] Jacobs. Wit. Albert Stuart. *Referred.*
Alfred Jacobs v. Margaret Ann Jacobs. Be it remembered that heretofore, to wit: on the 12th day of July 1848, in the clerk's office of the court aforesaid, came the plaintiff and filed in writing a statement of causes for divorce...He respectfully states, that he was lawfully married to his said wife Margaret Ann sometime in the month of December in the year 1841 that for several years after their marriage they lived together in the utmost harmony, that during that time he had issue by his said wife,

---

[16] This type of divorce completely dissolves the marriage, and makes it void from the beginning, the causes of it being precedent to the marriage. The parties may marry again. Upon the divorce of a man and his wife, equity will not assist the wife in recovering dower, at the husband's death, but shall leave her to the law.
[17] Acts of the General Assembly, 1849-1850, Chapter 328, "An ACT divorcing Alfred Jacobs from his wife Margaret Ann," passed January 23, 1850, p. 229.

two children, to wit: Ann Virginia born in the year 1843, and Sarah Elizabeth born in the year 1845, that during the said period of time he always treated his said wife with the utmost kindness, and provided her liberally with all the necessaries of life, that notwithstanding about three years ago, to wit: sometime in the year 1845, his said wife Margaret Ann deserted him and commenced a career of open and notorious prostitution, and that without the slightest cause or provocation on the part of the said Alfred, since the said Alfred avers and can prove that before the commencement of her criminal conduct, he had at all times after their marriage treated his said wife with uniform kindness and attention. And the said Alfred Jacobs further states, that even after his said wife Margaret Ann had begun to conduct herself as a prostitute, he exercised the utmost forbearance towards her and actually received her into his house; that after that she again deserted him and went to Washington City on a visit to some relations there; that whilst there she continued her course of prostitution, and as the said Alfred avers and can prove, contracted the venereal disease. The said Alfred further states, that his said wife has at all times utterly neglected her children, and that they are now under the care of his parents, with whom he himself resides, and also that his said wife still continues to conduct herself as an open and abandoned prostitute, by which causes, the said Alfred says, that his domestic happiness has been entirely destroyed, and his life rendered a burden to him. The said Alfred Jacobs, therefore prays the court, to cause a jury to be impaneled to ascertain the facts set forth in the above statement and that their verdict may be recorded. Witness my hand this 11th day of July 1848. Signed, Alfred [his mark] Jacobs. Wit. James Quaid.

In the matter of Alfred Jacobs against Margaret Ann Jacobs for a divorce it is certified by the court that there was evidence to satisfy the mind of the court that the offenses charged were not committed by the procurement or with the connivance of the complainant, and that the same had not been forgiven, and that they occurred within the period of five years before the institution of the suit, and that the complainant had not been guilty of the same offenses charged against the defendant within five years next before the institution of this suit.

At another day, to wit, at a session of the circuit superior court of law and chancery continued and held for the county of Alexandria the 14th November 1849, cause the petition by his attorney Albert Stuart, Esq., and therein came a jury, to wit... We of the jury find that the facts of the within statement are true...

1849, December 17. Mary Ann Conway. Alexandria Petitions, Box D, #A585 (also see #A597)

Petitioner states that on the 28th day of April 1840, she was married to Andrew Jamieson Conway, a mate and since a sea captain, engaged in the merchant service, and that the marriage took place in the Town of Alexandria where both parties then resided, and where your petitioner has lived from her birth to the present time... Becoming unfortunate in his voyages, in about two years, after the marriage, his fortunes became totally wrecked. His conduct in the course of the transactions, which resulted in his ruin, as your petitioner afterwards learned, was not only highly indiscreet, but might be characterized in much harsher language, were not your petitioner restrained from so doing, in the reflection, that his exposure, further than is actually necessary for the purposes of this petition, may hereafter injuriously affect the innocent offspring of said Conway and your petitioner... About the month of

August 1842, they went on a visit to Washington, after being there a few days, the said Conway, under the pretext of having business in Baltimore, left your petitioner with the promise to return in a few days, and take her back to Alexandria where they were then residing. Violating his promise, by failing to return, he has from that period, now upwards of seven years, totally deserted and abandoned your petitioner. Signed, Mary Ann Conway. *Referred.*

1850, December 2. Eliza Jane Baare. Alexandria Petitions, Box E, #A598.

Petitioner seeks divorce from her husband Ferdinand Rudolph Baare,[18] who deserted her and returned to his home in Prussia, stating to his brother that he never expected to return to America and that he would apply to Prussian authorities for annulment of marriage on grounds of being liable to Prussian military service when married. Letters show Eliza Jane Fisher, daughter of Charles Fisher, was married in FEB 1847 in Washington, D.C.,[19] to Ferdinand R. Baare, by birth a Prussian of the town of Minden, by Rev. Gillis, minister of the Protestant Episcopal Church of England. In 1848, the husband wrote that he was now an established grocer of St. Louis, Missouri, and requested her to join him there, which she did in the summer of 1848, carrying with her their infant child about six months old (the issue of the marriage) who died shortly after her arrival at St. Louis. Certificates. *Referred.*

1850, December 2. Mary Ann Conway. Alexandria Petitions, Box E, #A597 (also see #A585).

Petitioner seeks divorce from her husband, Andrew J. Conway, because of his desertion, leaving her and an innocent child to mourn with her the loss of a father's care.[20] Petitioner was married in 1840 and lived happily with her husband until 1842 when he left her and has never returned. Affidavits of Edgar Snowden, John Muir, W. Harper, F. Middleton, Wm. N. Berkeley. Letters of John H. Brent and Washington T. Harper show Mary Vansant,[21] daughter of James Vansant, intermarried with Capt. Andrew Conway, both then of the town of Alexandria. *Referred.*

---

[18] Acts of the General Assembly, 1850-1851, Chapter 296, "An ACT divorcing Eliza Jane Baare from her husband Ferdinand R. Baare," passed January 20, 1851, p. 196.

[19] Wesley E. Pippenger, District of Columbia Marriage Licenses, Register 1, 1811-1858 (Westminster, Md.: Family Line Publications, 1994), pp. 18, 203, "Eliza Fisher to Ferdinand Rudolph Baare, 24 FEB 1847."

[20] Acts of the General Assembly, 1850-1851, Chapter 301, "An ACT divorcing Mary Ann Conway from her husband Andrew J. Conway," passed January 9, 1851, pp. 197-198.

[21] Thomas Michael Miller, Alexandria & Alexandria (Arlington) County, Virginia Minister Returns & Marriage Bonds, 1801-1852 (Bowie, Md.: Heritage Books, Inc., 1987), p. 68, "Andrew J. Conway & Mary Ann VanZant, 27 APR 1840, bondsmen Andrew J. Conway, Andrew J. Fleming."

INDEX

A

abandonment, 1, 36, 74
abandonment and desertion, 73
Accomack Co., Va., 10, 18, 78, 98, 106, 108, 109
accoutrements, 64
Adams
    Martha Ann (Burruss), 79
    Thompson, 79
Adjutant General's Office, 26
Alabama, 50, 71
Alamance, Battle of, 19
Albemarle Co., Va., 43, 56, 95, 109, 111
alcoholics, 110
Alderton
    Margaret, 94
Alexander
    Amelia M., 45
    John, 45
Alexandria Co., Va., 96, 111
Alexandria Gazette, 107
Alexandria, Va., 4, 93, 99, 100, 105, 107, 112, 113
aliens, 7, 39, 42, 49, 50, 72, 86, 113
alimony, 25, 95
Alison
    Ann, 9
Alleghany Co., Va., 97, 110
Allen
    Julius C., 58
    Mahlon, 87
    Rebecca, 87
    Samuel, Col., 23
    Susan M. (Eaton), 58
    William, 57
Allison
    Elenorah A. (Neff), 68
    James G., 87
    Lemuel R., 68
    Martha A., 87
Alricks
    Ann (Peyton), 14
    West, 14
Alvis
    Mary (Walkley), 51
    Peter M., 51
Amelia Co., Va., 37, 108, 110
Amherst Co., Va., 64, 107, 110
anchors, 15

Anderson
    Ciceley, 2
    Nancy (Conn), 30
    Peter, 52
    Richard, 52
    William, 2
    William R., 30
Andrews
    Mary, 22
    Robert, 22
Angus
    George, 76
    Henry, 76
    Judith, 76
Apperson
    Sally, 107
Appleby
    William Crittenden, 53
Arell
    Christiana, 4
    David, 4, 107
    Phebe (Caverley), 107
    Richard, 4
    Samuel, 4
Arlington
    John, 98
Armstrong
    Elizabeth, 68
    Lewis W., 68
    Mary Anne, 68
    Virginia, 68
    William, 68
Arragan
    David, 50
Attorneys, 4, 9, 112
Auditor of Public Accounts, 2, 4-6, 8, 9, 12, 14, 15, 19, 21, 24-26, 29, 32, 34, 38, 43, 44, 51, 54, 62, 64, 75, 79, 93, 105
Augusta Co., Va., 40, 54, 71, 95, 108, 109

B

Baare
    Eliza Jane (Fisher), 99, 113
    Ferdinand R., 99
    Ferdinand Rudolph, 113
Bagent
    Eleanor, 77
    Jacob, 77

Bailey
    Absalom, 52
    Hannah S., 79
    Leonard G., 79
Ball
    Mary A., 71
Ballinger
    Richard, 70
    Sally (Wade), 70
Balls
    Caroline Octavia (Hodgson), 99
    Robert M., 99
Baltimore, Md., 29, 113
Barnes
    John, 66
    Lilly (Heldridge), 66
    William, 107
barracks, 25
Bartlam
    Temperance, 77
    William, 77
Bassett
    Burwell, Col., 26
bastard children, 61, 108, 110, 112
Bath Co., Va., 107, 108
Batte
    John H., 79
    Margaret D., 79
Battle of Point Pleasant, 32
battles
    Brandywine, 4
Baylis
    Rebecca (Birch), 109
    William P., 109
Bayliss
    Rebecca (Birch), 62
    William P., 62
Bayne
    Griffin, 13
    Nancy (Turner), 13
    Nancy J., 13
Beach
    Elizabeth, 15
Beard
    Amelia H., 93
    John H., 93
Beazley
    Ann Rebecca, 99
    Isaac M., 99
Bedford Co., Va., 13, 41, 70, 97, 110

Been
  Elizabeth, 18
Beeton
  Hannah H., 109
  Robert, 109
Belisle
  George, 79
Bell
  Fielding, 59
  Francina, 89
  Susan W. (Jarratt), 59
Bently
  Thomas, 52
Berkeley
  Julia, 35
  Robert, Dr., 35
  Wm. N., 113
Berkeley Co., Va., 22, 46
Bibby
  Cynthia, 52
Biddle
  Delana, 90
  Henry, 90
bigamist, 108
Binns
  Edmund, 110
  Elizabeth Ann, 110
Birch
  Rebecca, 62, 109
Birch creek, 55
Birdsong
  Amasa, 46
Black
  David, 12
  David, Dr., 12
Blackburn
  Sarah (Chapel), 87
  William H., 87
Blackburne
  Benjamin, 6
Blain
  Margaret, 39
  William, 39
Blankinship
  Ann T. (Potter), 99
  Thomas R., 99
Blood
  Fleming, 93
  Friendless, 93
  Moody, 111
  Olimpia (Meredith), 111
Blue Ridge mountains, 41
boarding, 20
Boisseau
  Mr., 48
Bolling
  Linnaeus, 23

bonds, 2, 33, 34, 36, 64, 92
Bonner
  Williamson, 33
Booth
  James, Capt., 62
Boothe
  James, Capt., 58
Bosher
  Charles, 11
  Susanna (Wingoe), 11
Boso
  John, 52
Botetourt Co., Va., 39, 84
Bott
  Susan C., 72
bounty lands, 21
Bowen
  Jefferson, 71
Boyd
  Lucy Gray Edmunds, 43
  William, 43
Brabstone
  William, 4
Brady
  Mary (Edrington), 36
  Thornton, 36
Brandywine, Battle of, 4
Bray
  Ann, 63
Breeden
  William, 11
Brent
  John H., 113
Brewer
  Delilah, 109
  John H., 109
brigantines, 15
Bright
  Lydia, 8
British
  wounded by, 19
British spy, 108
Brittain
  Elizabeth, 56
Brizendine
  Martha, 80
Brooke
  Helen A.W., 81
Brooke Co., Va., 64
Brough
  Margaret (Robertson), 13
  Thomas, 13
Brown
  Hugh, 32
  James, 62
  John, 107
  Lodwich, 55

Margaret (Haggerty), 107
Maria, 32
Orlando W., 88
Scotty Catharine, 88
Thomas, 64
Bruce
  Alexander, 11
  Andrew, 60, 61
  Charles, 60, 61
  George, 60
  Hannibal, 60, 61
  Isaac, 60, 61
  Jacob, 60
  Mary, 60
  Mildred "Milly", 60
  Rebecca, 60, 61
  Sarah, 60, 61
  Solomon, 60
Brunswick Co., Va., 47
brutality, 110
Buckingham
  Elisha, 88
  Ruth, 88
Buckingham Co., Va., 23, 38,
  46, 54, 77, 80, 98
Buckner
  Ariss, 28
  George M., 32
Bullock
  Lucy, 32
Burgess
  William, 14
Burke
  Mary, 29
  Michael, 29
Burruss
  Martha Ann, 79
Butler
  William R., 111
Butt
  Benjamin, Jr., 8
  Lydia, 8
  Lydia (Bright), 8
Butts
  Infants, 33
  Jesse, 33
  Jesse, heirs, 33
Byrd
  Francis Otway, 93

C

Cabell Co., Va., 19, 71, 86,
  90, 103
Calloway
  Cynthia A., 91
  James G., 91

Calvin
  John W., 50
Campbell
  Ann (Alison), 9
  Ann Maria (Oliver), 80
  John J., 80
  Robert, 9
Campbell Co., Va., 77
Caroline Co., Va., 6, 56
Carroll
  Tabitha T., 41
Carson
  Alonzo B., 49
  Augustus E., 49
  Caroline M., 49
  Egbert W., 49
  Emily G., 49
  George, 49
  George, children, 49
  Malvina W., 49
  Theophilus R., 49
Carter
  Cassius, 28
  Charles, 28
  Edward, 28
  James Broadnax, 43
  Jane, 109
  Jane Maria, 43
  John, 28
  John Hill, 28
  John Michell, 43
  Landon, 28
  Lucy Gray Edmunds, 43
  Rebecca Broadnax, 43
  Shirley, 28
  Thomas, 43
  Thomas, heirs, 43
Cassagrande
  Angela, 88
  Bertholomew, 88
Cauffman
  Rachael, 45
  Simon, 45
Cave
  Sophia, 108
Caverley
  Joseph, 107
  Peter, 4
  Phebe, 107
certificates, 14, 15
Chandler
  Richard, 78
Chapel
  Sarah, 87
Charles City Co., Va., 61, 68
Charlotte Co., Va., 19
Charlottesville, Va., 10

Chesterfield Co., Va., 43, 50,
  51, 77
Chiles
  Sarah, 56
Christian
  Sarah W., 61
Clarke Co., Va., 93, 102
Clayton
  Milly, 31
  William, 31
Clements
  Charles, 5
Clerks, 1
Clermont
  William Allen, Col., 57
Clopton
  Abner W., 16
  Sally B. (Warwick), 16
Cloud
  Mary, 70
  William, 70
Cole.
  John, 43
  Pamelia B., 43
Coleman
  Thomas, 52
Collins
  Elizabeth, 82
Combs
  Benjamin, 100
  Margaret A. (Edrington),
    100
Commandant
  37th Regiment, 25
commissary general, 64
Commissioners, 11, 28, 32,
  38
conduct, 54
Conn
  Nancy, 30
Conway
  Andrew J., 100, 113
  Andrew Jamieson, 112
  Mary (Vansant), 113
  Mary Ann, 100, 112, 113
Cook
  Elizabeth (Been), 18
  John, 18
Cooke
  John, Sr., 60
Cool
  Elizabeth, 102
Corbin
  Elizabeth, 67
Cortney
  John, 17
  Michael, 17

  Robert, 17
  Thomas, 17
counties
  Accomack, 18, 78, 98,
    106, 108, 109
  Albemarle, 43, 56, 95, 109,
    111
  Alexandria, 96, 111
  Alleghany, 97, 110
  Amelia, 37, 108, 110
  Amherst, 64, 107, 110,
    111
  Augusta, 40, 54, 71, 95,
    107-109
  Bath, 107, 108
  Bedford, 41, 70, 97, 110
  Berkeley, 22, 46
  Botetourt, 39, 84
  Brooke, 64, 65
  Brunswick, 47
  Buckingham, 23, 38, 46,
    54, 77, 80, 98
  Cabell, 19, 71, 86, 90, 103
  Campbell, 77
  Caroline, 6, 56
  Charles City, 68
  Charlotte, 19
  Chesterfield, 43, 50, 51, 77
  Clarke, 93, 102
  Culpeper, 53
  Cumberland, 34
  Dinwiddie, 48
  Essex, 80
  Fairfax, 1, 20, 62, 87, 105,
    109
  Fauquier, 27, 50
  Fayette, 88
  Fluvanna, 5
  Franklin, 59
  Frederick, 35, 45
  Goochland, 91, 98
  Grayson, 68, 80, 88
  Greenbrier, 35, 81, 102
  Greensville, 33
  Halifax, 33, 34, 45, 55
  Hampshire, 68, 83, 102
  Hanover, 2, 103
  Hardy, 60, 61, 67
  Harrison, 49, 67, 82, 84
  Henrico, 3, 39, 87, 96
  Henry, 7, 91
  Isle of Wight, 26, 27, 44,
    109, 110
  Jackson, 78
  James City, 61
  Jefferson, 93
  Kanawha, 5

116

King & Queen, 92
King George, 2
King William, 11, 42, 67, 69, 93, 110, 111
Lee, 56
Lewis, 58
Logan, 92
Loudoun, 77, 90
Louisa, 3, 31, 67, 68
Lunenburg, 20
Marion, 75, 84, 89
Marshall, 87, 95, 98
Mecklenburg, 96
Monongalia, 15
Montgomery, 10, 54
Morgan, 58, 94
Nansemond, 46, 63, 108-111
Nelson, 54, 80, 84
New Kent, 59, 61, 107, 109
Nicholas, 32, 89
Norfolk, 55, 103
Northampton, 22, 23, 74, 108, 110
Northumberland, 25
Nottoway, 21, 37, 101
Orange, 37, 69, 79
Page, 99
Patrick, 38, 79, 99
Pittsylvania, 54, 55, 91
Powhatan, 24, 57, 65, 66
Preston, 90
Prince Edward, 71
Prince George, 5, 31, 48
Prince William, 1, 11, 28, 107, 108
Princess Anne, 78
Pulaski, 83
Randolph, 96
Rappahannock, 71, 82
Ritchie, 82
Rockbridge, 62, 75
Rockingham, 74, 89, 95
Russell, 6
Scott, 97
Shenandoah, 88
Smyth, 69
Southampton, 86, 110
Spotsylvania, 32, 81, 97
Stafford, 57, 60, 100
Surry, 57, 65, 82, 111
Sussex, 46
Taylor, 82, 104
Tazewell, 58
Tyler, 76, 90
Washington, 28, 30

Wayne, 91, 103
Westmoreland, 44
Wood, 22, 52
Wyoming, 101
Wythe, 53
York, 24, 63
Court of Enquiry, 26
Cousins
    Charles, 37
Cowper
    Ann P.P., 27
    Anne P.P., 27
    William, 27
Cox
    Sarah E., 80
creditors, 9
crimes, 8
    adultery, 1, 19, 24, 36, 64, 70, 73, 107-109, 111
    bigamy, 27, 30, 31, 33, 36, 37, 51, 73, 92
    desertion, 107
    felony, 79, 108
    forgery, 94, 110
    horse-stealing, 64, 109
    murder, 2, 29, 35, 111
    theft, 110
Crittenden
    William, 53
Cropp
    Eliza F., 57
    Robert, 57
Cross
    Solomon, 52
Crow
    Amanda, 77
    Samuel M., 77
cruelty, 19, 108, 109
Culpeper Co., Va., 53
Cumberland Co., Va., 34
Cunningham
    Phebe, 62
    Thomas, 62

D

damages, 25
Dantignac
    Ann (Peachy), 1
    John, 1
Danville, Va., 91
Davis
    Elias, 88
    Huldah, 88
    Peter C., 80
    Sarah E. (Cox), 80

de Tubeuf
    Alexander, 6
    Francis, 6
    Peter Francis, 6
    Peter Francis, heirs of, 6
Dean
    Betsy, 107
    Betty, 17
    Billy, 17
    Daphney, 17
    Elizabeth, 107
    Frankey, 17
    Henry, 17
    John, 17
debts, 3, 20
Depp
    Abraham, 57
    John, 57
desertion, 108, 110-113
Dewey
    Joseph, 52
Dibrell
    Anthony, 23
Dick
    Anne, 26
    David, 26
    David, Dr., heirs, 26
    Samuel, 26
    Wardrope, 26
Dinwiddie Co., Va., 48
District of Columbia, 20
divorces, 84, 107-110, 112
    act concerning, 73, 76
    Adams, Thompson, 79
    Alexander, John, 45
    Allen, Julius C., 58
    Allen, Mahlon, 87
    Allison, James G., 87
    Allison, Lemuel R., 68
    Alricks, West, 14
    Alvis, Peter M., 51
    Anderson, William R., 30
    Baare, Ferdinand R., 99, 113
    Bagent, Jacob, 77
    Bailey, Leonard G., 79
    Ballinger, Richard, 70
    Balls, Robert M., 99
    Barnes, John, 66
    Bartlam, William, 77
    Batte, John H., 79
    Bayliss, William P., 62
    Bayne, Griffin, 13
    Beard, John H., 93
    Beazley, Isaac M., 99
    Bell, Fielding, 59
    Biddle, Henry, 90

117

Blackburn, William H., 87
Blankinship, Thomas R., 99
Bosher, Charles, 11
Brady, Thornton, 36
Brough, Thomas, 13
Brown, Hugh, 32
Brown, Orlando W., 88
Buckingham, Elisha, 88
Burke, Michael, 29
Butt, Benjamin, Jr., 8
Calloway, James G., 91
Campbell, John J., 80
Campbell, Robert, 9
Cassagrande, Berth., 88
Cauffman, Simon, 45
Clopton, Abner W., 16
Cloud, William, 70
Cole, John, 43
Combs, Benjamin, 100
Conway, Andrew J., 100, 112
Cook, John, 18
Cowper, William, 27
Crow, Samuel M., 77
Dantignac, John, 1
Davis, Elias, 88
Davis, Peter C., 80
Dobyns, Jonah, 30
Drinkwater, Robert E., 101
Du Veyriere, Balthazar S., 102
Edmunds, John W.A., 65
Eubank, Alfred, 67
Evans, Ephraim, 70
Falkler, Cutlip, 89
Ferte, Felix, 55
Fleece, John E., 94
Foster, George W., 89
Fouch, Isaac, 15
Foulkes, John A., 45
Gay, Charles, 46
Goddard, Jared N., 95
Gosling, Palmer, 81
Grandstaff, John, 71
Grantham, Uriah, 31
Gresham, Joseph, 61
Hall, Richard B., 69
Hamilton, Robert S., 81
Harper, Watkins, 80
Harris, George W., 100
Heiskell, Ferdinand S., 95
Heyden, George, 69
Hillary, William, 82
Hilliard, Benjamin, 101
Howell, John, 89
Hughes, Thomas, 82

Huston, Robert, 67
Hutchings, David W., 75
Jacobs, Alfred, 96, 112
Johnson, John C., 101
Johnston, George, 101
Jones, George, 101
Jones, James R., 82
Jones, Richard, 22
Keblinger, David, 95
Kellum, Benjamin, 63
Kerns, Jacob, 75
Kimberlin, Martin, 14
Kirk, John B., 67
Knight, Walton, 19
Lane, George W., 82
Latham, Ayres, 10
Leatherman, Abraham George, 83
Lewis, Manuel, 96
Luck, James C., 56
Lynch, James, 53
M'Ginty, Daniel, 89
Magee, Hugh, 58
Martin, James M., 74
Mills, Alexander W., 56
Mills, Martin L., 43
Mitchell, Robert H., 91
Moffett, John, 74
Moody, Ishmael, 44
Moore, Henry C., 96
Moran, Robert, 84
Mosby, Hezekiah, 24
Myers, William R., 83
Newby, Henry, 96
Newton, Abraham, 27
Norman, James B., 91
Odell, Stephen, 83
Owen, Leonard, 16
Ownby, Edward, 97
Pannill, Edmund, 69
Parker, David, 46
Pettus, Dabney, 8
Pettus, Hugh M., 36
Peyton, John, 90
Phipps, David C., 80
Plum, Jacob, 90
Polling, Joseph S., 102
Prickett, Thomas, 76
Rankin, Abner G., 54
Raymond, Henry P., 91
Roane, Newman B., 42
Roberts, Nathaniel G., 102
Robertson, John A., 21
Rollins, Henry, 97
Rose, Daniel, 11
Rucker, William, 97
Simpson, William, 54

Sims, Hugh S., 40
Sims, Robert, 83
Smith, Hiram alias Highland, 72
Spencer, William B., 97
Stephens, Henry L., 102
Stephens, James M., 98
Terry, William B., 98
Thomas, Francis, 81
Thurman, George B., 77
Toler, William B., 41
Trueman, John, 51
Warden, Malachi, 78
Warner, Osborn, 23
Watson, Richard P., 71
Watts, James L., 64
Williams, John W., 92
Williams, William B., 59
Wilson, John, 46, 102
Woodyard, John, 84
Woolfolk, Bentley B., 103
Wright, Benjamin, 78
Wright, Shelton, 84
Yonson, William, 90
Dixon
  James, 3
  James, heirs, 3
  John, 3
  Lucy, 3
  Nancy, 3
  Patsey, 3
  Sarah, 3
Dobyns
  Jonah, 30
  Sopha (Leftwich), 30
Dodson
  George, 54
Douglass
  George, 12
  Judy, 12
  Margaret, 12
Drake
  Louisa W., 109
  Robert, 109
Drewry
  William H., 65
Drinkwater
  Henrietta, 101
  Robert E., 101
drunkenness, 95, 109, 110
Du Veyriere
  Balthazar Sperat, 102
  Jane R., 102
Dumas
  Benjamin, 107
  Sally (Apperson), 107
Dumfries, Va., 108

Duncan
David, 15
Dunlap
Ellen (Shields), 108
Robert, 108
duplicate certificates, 12
Durell
James, 25
dwelling houses
occupied by troops, 25

E

Eager
Eliza Ann, 44
Eanes
George H., 110
Mary, 110
Easton
Sarah (Harrison), 21
Eaton
Susan M., 58
Edmunds
Ann (Kirk), 65
John W.A., 65
Edrington
Margaret A., 100
Mary, 36
Egborn
Delilah (Williams), 107
Jacob, 107
Elder
Thomas, 3
emancipation, 17, 18, 37, 60,
62, 63, 76, 78
England, 104
Engravers
reprint will of George
Washington, 106
Essex Co., Va., 80
Eubank
Alfred, 67
Ann (Taylor), 110
Ann Eliza, 67
Evans
Anna, 3
Ephraim, 70
Jane L. (Wadsworth), 70
Ewing
John D., Rev., 62

F

Fairfax
Henry, Capt., 93, 105
Fairfax Co., Va., 1, 20, 62,

87, 109
Clerk of County Court, 105
Falkler
Cutlip, 89
Francina (Bell), 89
Falmouth, Va., 64
Farley
Alice E., 50
Philip, 50
farms, 28
father of 34 children, 47
Fauquier Co., Va., 27, 50
Fayette Co., Va., 88
feme sole, 1, 27, 30, 94
Fergusson
John, 39
Ferrell
Robert, 15
Ferte
Felix, 55
Sarah (Waterman), 55
Field
Sarah, 71
Finney
Elizabeth A., 108
William W., 98
Fisher
Ann, 54
Charles, 113
Eliza Jane, 99, 113
Mr., 48
Fleece
John E., 94
Margaret (Alderton), 94
Fleet
Rebecca Jane, 102
Fleming
Andrew J., 113
Flinn
Jacob, 52
John, 52
Floyd
Frank, 17
Mitchel, 17
Samuel, 17
Fluvanna Co., Va., 5
forfeitures, 18
Foster
George W., 89
Margaret M., 89
Fouch
Elizabeth (Beach), 15
Isaac, 15
Foulkes
John A., 45
Franklin Co., Va., 59
Frederick Co., Va., 35, 45

Fredericksburg, Va., 32, 108
Superior Court of
Chancery, 28, 47
French emigrants, 6
Fulton
Mr., 8
Rebecca, 8

G

Gaines
William, 19
Gardner
Overton T., 67
Pamelia M., 67
Gates's defeat, 31
Gauder
Frederick, 10
Gay
Amasa, 46
Charles, 46
Macy (Birdsong), 46
Gee
James S., 76
George
Hannah, 16
Samuel, 16
Gibbon
Thomas, 33
Gill
Sarah (Paddleford), 108
Thomas, 108
Gilliam
James S., Dr., 48, 49
Robert, 48
Theophilus F., 48
Gillis
Rev., 113
Gilmer
George, 7
George, children of, 7
Gilpin
John, 52
Glenn
Sarah Ann, 91
Goddard
Jared N., 95
Martha, 95
Godwin
Edmond, 109
Jane D., 109
Goochland Co., Va., 91, 98
Goodrich
John, the elder, 14
Goodwin
Jos'h, 48

119

Gosling
    Amanda, 81
    Palmer, 81
Governors
    Virginia, 13, 93
Grandstaff
    John, 71
    Susan, 71
Grantham
    Sarah C., 31
    Uriah, 31
Gray
    Joseph, 39
    Margaret (Blain), 39
    Nancy, 27
Grayson Co., Va., 68, 80, 88
Great Britain, 41, 49
Green
    Duff, 64
Greenbrier Co., Va., 35, 81,
    102
Greensville Co., Va., 33
Gresham
    Joseph, 61
    Sarah W. (Christian), 61
Griffin
    Thomas, 63
Griffith
    John, 22
Grocers, 113
guardians, 4, 20, 33, 50, 52,
    56
gun powder
    explosion, 25
Gunnell
    Joshua C., 105
Gunners, 2

H

Haggerty
    Margaret, 107
Hagood
    William R., 55
Halifax Co., Va., 33, 55
Hall
    Richard B., 69
    Sarah (Paul), 69
Hamilton
    George, 32
    Helen A.W. (Brooke), 81
    Robert S., 81
Hampshire Co., Va., 68, 83,
    102
Hampton
    Nancy, 16

Haney
    Elizabeth, 101
Hanover Co., Va., 2, 103
Hanway
    Samuel, 17
Hardy Co., Va., 60, 61, 67
Harman
    Elias V., 58
    Matthias, 58
Harmer
    George, 7
Harper
    Martha (Brizendine), 80
    W., 113
    Washington T., 113
    Watkins, 80
Harris
    Cherry Tyas, 86
    George W., 100
    James, 110
    John, Capt., 14
    Lewis, 86
    Martha Ann, 86
    Martha C. (Hemmings),
    110
    Mary E.S., 100
Harrison
    Benjamin, 50, 68
    Dorothy, 21
    Dorothy Jones, 37
    Henry, 37, 68
    John Page, 68
    Margaret S., 50
    Polly Jones, 37
    Randolph, 48
    Robert Hanson, Lt. Col.,
    21
    Sarah, 21
Harrison Co., Va., 49, 67, 82,
    84
Hasty
    Nancy D., 82, 111
    Robert, 111
Hawthorn
    Alexander, 15
    Robert, 15
Hayes
    Henry, 75
Heath
    Jane (Paulean), 72
    William, 72
Heiskell
    Ferdinand S., 95
    Huldah (Graham), 95
Heldridge
    Lilly, 66

Hemmings
    John, 110
Henderson
    Elizabeth (Irwin), 9
    Lilburn L., 28
Hening
    William Waller, iii, 12
Henrico Co., Va., 3, 39, 87,
    96
Henry Co., Va., 7, 91
Herris
    Edward, 105
Heyden
    George, 69
    Mary Anne (Weddell), 69
Hill
    Cordelia (Thurman), 111
    Henry, 37
    Judith, 107
    William, 107
    William F., 111
Hillary
    Catharine (Withers), 82
    William, 82
Hilliard
    Benjamin, 101
    Mary A. (Lydick), 101
Hinchman
    Ulysses, 92
Hodgson
    Caroline Octavia, 99
Holcombe
    William I., Dr., 110
Hones
    Joseph, 14
Hopkins
    William, 104
Hopper
    Catharine, 44
    Eliza Ann (Eager), 44
    Matthew, 44
Hornbarger
    Nancy, 54
horses, 29
Houchins
    Edward, 31
Howard
    Ann H., 65
    Betsy (Dean), 107
    Jane C., 65
    Joseph, 52, 65, 66
    Maria, 65
    Mary, 65
    Richard H., 65
    William, 65, 107
Howell
    John, 89

Maria, 89
Howle
Jacqueline P., 61
Martha C., 61
Mary C., 61
Matilda A., 61
Howlett
Thomas, 37
Hubard
James T., 23
Susanna, 23
Hughes
John S., 71
Lucinda (Harrison), 82
Thomas, 82
Hughlett
Robert W., 25
Roger W., children, 25
husband of 4 wives, 47
Huston
Elizabeth (Corbin), 67
Robert, 67
Hutchings
David W., 75
Elizabeth C., 75

I

idiocy, 73
illegitimate children, 8, 69, 72
Illinois department, 15
Illinois regiment, 15
Illinois territory, 18
indemnification, 34
Indians, 5, 62
Innes
Mary Ann, 49
insane, 65
insolvents, 64
intoxication, 95
Ireland, 39, 42
Irwin
Elizabeth, 9
James, 9
John, Jr., 9
Robert, heirs, 9
Isle of Wight Co., Va., 26, 27, 44, 109, 110

J

Jackson Co., Va., 78
Jacobs
Alfred, 96, 111, 112
Ann Virginia, 112
Hetty, 52

Margaret Ann, 96, 111, 112
Sarah Elizabeth, 112
Solomon, 52
jails, 94
James City Co., Va., 61
Jameson
Alexander, 5
Elizabeth, 5
Jarratt
Susan W., 59
Jefferson Co., Va., 93
Jeffries
Jeremiah, 44
Johns
John, 46
Johnson
Amanda, 84
Elizabeth (Haney), 101
John C., 101
William R., 48
Johnston
Absolem, 108
George, 101
Margaret, 108
Susannah, 101
Jones
Benjamin, 33
Dorothy, 37
Elizabeth (Collins), 82
George, 101
Israel, 110
James R., 82
Malinda S. (Topping), 101
Mary, 110
Peggy, 108
Polly, 37
Richard, 22, 108
Jourdan
Oney, 23
Joyner
Asahel, 110
Julia Ann (Reese), 110
judgments, 14
juries, 61, 75, 112
Northampton Co., Va., 22
Justice
Bowman, 18
Eve, 18
Peggy, 18
Robin, 18

K

Kalussowski
Henry, 86
Kanawha Co., Va., 5

Keblinger
David, 95
Elizabeth, 95
Keenan
James, 40
Wiliam, 40
Kellum
Ann (Bray), 63
Benjamin, 63
Kelly
John, 35
Nathaniel, 35
Polly, 35
Ker
Edward H., 106
Kerns
Jacob, 75
Mahala, 75
Kimberlin
Elizabeth (Sponsler), 14
Martin, 14
King & Queen Co., Va., 92
King George Co., Va., 2
King William Co., Va., 42, 67, 69, 93, 110, 111
court penalty, 11
Kirk
Ann, 65
John B., 67
Mary, 67
Knight
Anne H., 19
Walton, 19
Korwin
Henry, 86

L

Lackland
John James, 98
Lambert
John, 7
Lamkin
Elizabeth Lewis, 20
Jane Cross, 20
Mary Sharp, 20
Peter, Col., 20
Peter, orphans of, 20
Sharp, 20
Sharp, estate, 20
land, 15
Alexandria, Va., 105
Bedford Co., Va., 41
Botetourt Co., Va., 39
bounty, 21
Buckingham Co., Va., 23
Caroline Co., Va., 6, 7

Charlottesville, Va., 10
deeds, 17, 28, 72, 103
Dinwiddie Co., Va., 48
division, 33, 38, 49
escheated, 2, 3, 7, 9, 10,
  17, 35
Greensville Co., Va., 33
Halifax Co., Va., 33
Harrison Co., Va., 49
Henrico Co., Va., 39
Henry Co., Va., 7
Isle of Wight Co., Va., 26
Lunenburg Co., Va., 20
Mary Jane, 63
Monongalia Co., Va., 17
North Carolina, 38
patents, 17, 52
Petersburg, Va., 12
Powhatan Co., Va., 65
Prince George Co., Va., 48
Russell Co., Va., 6
Spotsylvania Co., Va., 32
Taylor Co., Va., 104
Wayne Co., Va., 103
Wood Co., Va., 52
Lane
  George W., 82, 111
  Nancy D. (Hasty), 82, 111
last will and testaments, 3, 6,
  7, 17, 41, 47, 48, 50,
  52, 54, 55, 57, 59, 60,
  105
  nuncupative, 72
  original removed, 105, 106
Latham
  Ayres, 10
  Tabitha, 10
Lawrence
  John, 104
Laws of the Commonwealth
  published by Hening, 12
leases, 4
Leatherman
  Abraham George, 83
  Mary Ellen, 83
Lee Co., Va., 56
Leftwich
  Sopha, 30
legislative petitions, 107
Leonard
  Robert, 4
Lester
  Rachel, 110
Lewis
  Andrew, Col., 32
  Ann, 96
  Elizabeth A. (Finney), 108

Manuel, 96
  Stephen J., 108
Lewis Co., Va., 58
licenses, 11, 71, 108
Lightfoot
  Indiana, 69
  John, 69
  Josiah, 69
  Mary E., 69
  Miss, 69
Literary Fund, 31, 35, 39, 41,
  42, 49, 50, 52, 103-105
Littlepage
  Ann H. (Howard), 65
loans, 6
Logan Co., Va., 92
lots
  for rent, Alexandria, Va., 4
Loudoun Co., Va., 77, 90
Louisa Co., Va., 3, 31, 67, 68
Lower
  Peter, 103
Lowry
  Aaron, 67
  Mary, 67
  Overton T., 67
  Pamelia M., 67
Lucas
  Peggy, 62
  Scipio, 62
Luck
  James C., 56
  Sarah, 56
  Sarah (Chiles), 56
lumber houses, 25, 42
lunatics, 26, 32, 53
Lunenburg Co., Va., 20
Lydick
  Mary A., 101
Lynch
  Elizabeth, 53
  James, 53
  William, Sr., 47
Lynchburg, Va., 101
Lyon
  Alexander, 107
  Judith (Hill), 107

M

M'Cormick
  Thomas Winston, 46
M'Craw
  Catharine, 68
  Raleigh, 68
  Sally, 68

M'Dowell
  Sarah C.P., 81
M'Farland
  Ezekiel, 52
M'Ginty
  Daniel, 89
  Louisa (Roberts), 89
M'Graw
  Charles, 6
M'Lemore
  Cherry Tyas, 86
  Martha Ann, 86

Mabry
  Nathaniel, 33
Magee
  Andrew, 42
  George, 42
  Hannah (Thornburgh), 58
  Hugh, 58
  John, 42
man of colour, 16, 24, 37, 57,
  62, 76, 109
Mann
  Elizabeth, 5
  Thomas, 5
Marion Co., Va., 75, 84, 89
marriages, 23, 44, 56, 57, 92,
  94, 107-110
  after divorce, 101
  anulled, 75, 94
  to dead wife's sister, 108
Marshall
  Humphrey, 51
  James E., 20
  James E., orphans, 20
  James Elgin, 20
Marshall Co., Va., 87, 95, 98
Marteney
  William, 32
Martin
  James M., 74
  Mr., 8
  Rebecca, 74
Marx
  Joseph, 52
Maryland, 20
  removal to, 22
Mason
  Edmund, 33
  Peyton, 48
Mayors
  Richmond, Va., 6
McCandlish
  Robert, 26
McCaughen
  Charles, 108

Sophia, 108
Sophia (Cave), 108
McCord
  Elizabeth, Mrs., 95
McCreery
  John, 42
  John, children, 42
  Mary, 42
Meade
  Richard Kidder, Lt. Col., 21
Mecklenburg Co., Va., 96
Medlin
  Jane, 49
Meek
  Martha, 107
merchant service, 112
Merchants, 112
Meredith
  Fleming, 93
  Friendless, 93
  Olimpia, 111
Merryman
  Betsy, 24
Metcalf
  Elizabeth, 96
Methodist Church, 95
Middleton
  F., 113
military, 5, 38, 62, 75, 93, 105
  103rd Regiment, 65
  37th Regiment, 25
  45th Regiment, 64
  68th Regiment, 26
  Continental line, 21
  officers, 21
  Virginia line, 6, 38, 44, 51
militia, 25
militia fines, 26, 64
Miller
  Jane, 46, 109
  Thomas Michael, 113
Mills
  Alexander W., 56
  Elizabeth, 43, 109
  Elizabeth (Brittain), 56
  Martin L., 43
  Martin S., 109
Minden, Prussia, 113
mines, 55
Ministers, 44, 92, 108
Mississippi Territory, 22
Missouri, 65
Mitchell
  Benjamin, 52
  Mary A., 91
  Robert H., 91

Moffett
  John, 74
  Sally, 74
Monongalia Co., Va., 15, 17
Montgomery Co., Va., 10, 54
Moody
  Eliza Ann (Eager), 44
  Ishmael, 44
Moore
  Elizabeth (Metcalf), 96
  Henry C., 96
  Stephen, Capt., 107
  William, 38
  William, heirs, 38
Moran
  Lydia (Poe), 84
  Robert, 84
Morgan
  Levy, Lt., 75
Morgan Co., Va., 58, 94
Morgan town, Va., 15
Morris
  Edward, 108
  Elizabeth, 8
  Rhoda, 108
Morriss
  George Whitfield, 59
  George Whitfield, Dr., 59
  James T., 59
Mortimore
  Welford, 109
Mosby
  Betsy (Merryman), 24
  Hezekiah, 24
Moss
  Alfred, 105
  Margaret, 63
Mount
  Thomas C., 47
  William, 47
  William, devisees, 47
Muir
  John, 113
  William H., 105
Mulatto children, 8, 10, 11,
  27, 61, 108
Mulattoes, 60, 61, 78
Munford
  William, 12
Myers
  Virginia (Pollard), 83
  William R., 83

N

name changes
  Allen, William, 57

Arlington, John, 98
Armstrong, Elizabeth, 68
Armstrong, Lewis W., 68
Armstrong, Mary Anne, 68
Armstrong, Virginia, 68
Carroll, Tabitha T., 41
Crittenden, William, 53
Drewry, William H., 65
Gardner, Overton T., 67
Gardner, Pamelia M., 67
Harman, Daniel H., 58
Harman, Elias V., 58
Harman, William Buse, 58
Harris, Cherry Tyas, 86
Harris, Martha Ann, 86
Harrison, Dorothy Jones,
  37
Harrison, Henry, 68
Harrison, Polly Jones, 37
Johns, Thomas Winston,
  46
Korwin, Henry, 86
Lackland, John James, 98
M'Dowell, Sarah C.P., 81
Meredith, Fleming, 93
Meredith, Friendless, 93
Morriss, George Whitfield,
  59
Newman, Henry, 37
Patteson, David, 54
Poindexter, Jacqueline
  Lewis, 61
Poindexter, Martha C., 61
Poindexter, Mary C., 61
Poindexter, Matilda A., 61
Smith, Mary Jane, 63
Thompson, Catharine, 68
Thompson, Raleigh, 68
Thompson, Sally, 68
Upshur, George Littleton,
  74
Upshur, John Henry, 74
Wilson, Indiana, 69
Wilson, John, 69
Wilson, Josiah, 69
Wilson, Mary E., 69
Wingfield, Mary E.S., 101
Wood, Henry, 56
Nansemond Co., Va., 37, 46,
  63, 108-110
natural son, 3
naturalizations, 39, 86
Neal
  Charles, 10
  Elizabeth, 10
Neale
  James H., 52

Neff
Elenorah A., 68
Negroes, 16, 18, 19, 22, 34,
60, 61, 78, 108, 109
children, 22
Nelson Co., Va., 54, 80, 84
New Kent Co., Va., 59, 61,
109
New York, 44
New York, N.Y., 101
Newby
Frances W., 96
Henry, 96
Newman
Henry, 37
Newton
Abraham, 27
Nancyn (Gray), 27
Niblo
Eliza, 72
Nicholas
John, 38
Nicholas Co., Va., 32, 89
Nimmo
James, 14
Norfolk Co., Va., 55, 103
Norfolk, Va., 31, 102, 104
Norman
James B., 91
Lucy W., 91
North Carolina, 19, 38, 46,
109
Northampton Co., Va., 22, 74,
108, 110
Northumberland Co., Va., 25
Nottingham
Addison, 110
George Upshur, 74
John Henry, 74
Peggy, 110
Nottoway Co., Va., 21, 37,
101

O

oath of fidelity, 92
Odell
Eleanor, 83
Stephen, 83
Ogden
Noah, 52
Ohio, 74
Oliver
Ann Maria, 80
Cynthia L., 55
Elizabeth C., 55
Orange Co., Va., 37, 69, 79

Orgain
Richard Griffin, 57
William Griffin, 57
orphans, 20
Arell, David, of, 4
Orrey
James, 41
overseers of the poor, 19
Owen
Leonard, 16
Nancy (Hampton), 16
Ownby
Edward, 97
Elizabeth, 97

P

Paddleford
Sarah, 108
Page Co., Va., 99
Pannill
Edmund, 69
Elizabeth A., 69
Parker
David, 46, 109
James, 41
Jane (Carter), 109
Jane (Miller), 46, 109
John, 41
Moses, 41
Nancy, 41
Parsons
Joseph, 62
William I., 48
Patrick Co., Va., 38, 79, 99
Patteson
David, 54
David R., 54
Paul
Sarah, 69
Paulean
Jane, 72
Payne
Robert S., Dr., 110
Peachy
Ann, 1
Peery
John, 19
Pendleton
John, 14
Paulina, 84
penitentiaries, 79
Penn
Clarke, 79
Pennybacker
John, 52
pensioners, 2, 4, 5, 19, 31,

32, 38, 54, 58
discontinue, 6
persons of colour, 18, 37, 60
Peter
John, 48
Petersburg, Va., 12, 25, 29,
42, 48, 57, 72, 76
petitions, 107
Pettus
Barbara W. (Price), 36
Dabney, 8
Elizabeth, 8
Elizabeth (Morris), 8
Hugh M., 36
Peyton
Ann, 14
Delila (Sheff), 90
John, 90
Phipps
David C., 80
Dorcas (Stamper), 80
Pierce
Sarah, 111
Pippenger
Wesley E., 113
Pittenger
John, 64, 65
Pittman
Ann, 2
John, 2
Mary, 2
William, 2
William, heirs, 2
Pittsylvania Co., Va., 54, 55,
91
plantations, 48
Plum
Jacob, 90
Mary Jane, 90
Poe
Lydia, 84
Poindexter
Jacqueline Lewis, 61
Martha C., 61
Mary C., 61
Matilda A., 61
Point Pleasant, Battle of, 32
Poland, 86
Pollard
Ambrose, 53
George B., 53
Thomas G., 53
Virginia, 83
Polling
Elizabeth (Cool), 102
Joseph S., 102

124

Pope
Ann, 108
Jacquelin A., 108
Potter
Ann T., 99
Potts
John, 3
poverty, 108
Powell
Edward, 29
Walter, 87
Powhatan Co., Va., 24, 57,
65, 66
Preston Co., Va., 90
Price
Barbara W., 36
Prickett
Elizabeth, 76
Thomas, 76
Prince Edward Co., Va., 71
Prince George Co., Va., 5,
31, 48
Prince William Co., Va., 1, 11,
28, 107, 108
Princess Anne Co., Va., 78
prisons, 64, 79, 111
prostitutes, 107
Protestant Episcopal Church
of England, 113
Prussia, 113
Pulaski Co., Va., 83

Q
Quaid
James, 112
Quartermaster General, 15

R
Ragley
John, 110
Raincock
George, 104
Rebecca, 104
Rebecca, daughters, 104
Ramsey
Sally (Parker), 41
Randolph
Robert, 28
Thomas M., 64
Randolph Co., Va., 96
Rangers, 58, 75
Rankin
Abner G., 54
Ann (Fisher), 54

Rappahannock Co., Va., 71,
82
Rawls
Bryant, 110
Rachel (Lester), 110
Raymond
Henry P., 91
Sarah Ann (Glenn), 91
Reagh
Martha (Meek), 107
Robert, 107
Recorders
Court of Enquiry, 26
Reeder
Benjamin, 17
Reese
Julia Ann, 110
regimental court of enquiry,
65
religion, 36
retailing goods
without a license, 11, 71
Richerson
Joseph, 7
Richmond
John, 3
Richmond, Va., 6, 45, 52, 83,
88, 100, 101
Superior Court of
Chancery, 24
Riflemen, 64
rifles, 64
Riggan
William H., 65
Ritchie Co., Va., 82
Roane
Anna, 103
Evelina, 42
Newman B., 42
Robb
James, 7
Roberts
Louisa, 89
Mary A.E., 102
Nathaniel G, 102
Robertson
Alexander M., 49
Charles, 49
David, 49
Elizabeth, 21
George, Jr., 49
John A., 21
Margaret, 13
Mary, 49
Robinson
John, 104
Washington, heirs, 104

Rockbridge Co., Va., 62, 75
Rockingham Co., Va., 74, 89,
95
Rollins
Henry, 97
Susan, 97
Rose
Daniel, 11
Henrietta (White), 11
John N., 17
Margaret, 17
Ross
Ann Eliza, 110
Rucker
Elizabeth, 97
William, 97
Russell
Gervas E., 44
Hannah, 44
James L., 44
John, 44
John B., 44
Joshua, 44
Russell Co., Va., 6

S
School Commissioners, 71
schooling, 20
Scidmore
Andrew, 32
Scotland, 39
Scott
Christopher C., 33
Elizabeth R., 33
Francis T., 33
James, 15
James B., 33
John B., Gen., 33
John B., Gen., heirs, 33
John W., 33
Martha Ann, 33
Richard M., 20
Richard Marshall, 20
William T., 33
Scott Co., Va., 97
Semple
James, 12
Joanna, 12
separation from bed and
board, 76
Sergeants, 62
Shannon
William, 15
Sheets
Henry, 52
Michael, 52

William, 52
Sheff
 Delila, 90
Shenandoah Co., Va., 88
Shepheard
 David, 54
Shepherd
 Samuel, iii
Shepperd
 John, 5
Sheriffs, 2, 15, 64, 71, 79
Shields
 Ellen, 108
ships
 Henry Galley, 2
Shreve
 Mary Anne, 72
 Mr., 72
Shultz
 George, 109
 Susannah, 109
Siege of York, 38
Simmet
 Matthias, 35
 Nathaniel, 35
 Polly, 35
Simpson
 Nancy (Hornbarger), 54
 William, 54
Sims
 Hugh S., 40
 Mary Margaret, 83
 Rebecca, 40
 Robert, 83
Skipwith
 Mr., 48
slander, 110
slavery, 60
slaves, 18, 20, 22, 28, 29, 32,
  34, 35, 40, 50, 52, 53,
  60, 61, 76, 78
Sleeth
 David W., 62
 John, 62
Smith
 Anne, 68
 Elizabeth, 10, 68
 Frances, 24
 Highland, 72
 Hiram, 72
 James, 52
 Jane (Paulean), 72
 John, 24
 Lewis W., 68
 Mary Anne, 68
 Mary Jane, 63
 Virginia, 68

William, 10
Smithfield, Va., 26
Smyth Co., Va., 69
Snead
 Edward S., 106
 Peter, 78
Snowden
 Edgar, 113
soldiers, 4-6, 16, 19, 24, 31,
  54, 58
Somerset Co., Md., 106
South Carolina, 38
Southampton Co., Va., 86,
  110
Spencer
 Elizabeth, 97
 William B., 97
spirits, 71
Sponsler
 Elizabeth, 14
Spotsylvania Co., Va., 32, 81,
  97
Sprouse
 Henry, 56
St. Eustatia, 40
St. Louis, Mo., 113
St. Thomas, 40
Stafford Co., Va., 57, 60, 100
Stamper
 Dorcas, 80
Standard
 Rebecca Broadnax
  (Carter), 43
Starr
 Hezekiah, 29
Stephens
 Henry L., 102
 James M., 98
 Mary Ann, 98
 Rebecca Jane (Fleet), 102
Stewart
 John, 72
 Mary Anne, 72
Stith
 Griffin, 28
Storer
 Dorothy (Harrison), 21
streets
 Pitt, Alexandria, Va., 105
 Prince, Alexandria, Va.,
  105
 Royal, Alexandria, Va.,
  105
Stuart
 Albert, 111, 112
 Archibald, Jr., 18
 Nancy, 18

suicides, 18
suits, 73, 76
Surgeons, 43
Surry Co., Va., 57, 65, 82,
  111
suspending certain
  executions, 2
Sussex Co., Va., 46
Sutton
 Christopher, 41
swindler, 108, 110
Swinton
 Anna, 6, 7
 George, 6, 7
 James, 6, 7
swords, 93

T

Tanner
 Creed, devisees, 55
 Dorothy, 2
 Elizabeth, 55
 Jacob, 2
 John H., 55
Tate
 Mildred C., 59
Tatham (see Latham), 10
Tatsapaugh
 John, 93
taxes, 104
 arrears, 2
 delinquent, 104
 due, 15
 exempt from paying, 47
Taylor
 Ann, 110
 Creed, 12
 Edmund F., 20
 John, 20
 William H., 20
Taylor Co., Va., 82, 104
Tazewell Co., Va., 58
tenants, 48
tenants in common, 7
tenements, 35
Tennessee, 6, 28, 108
Terebee
 James, 14
Terry
 Mary J., 98
 William B., 98
Thomas
 Francis, 81
 Sarah C.P. (M'Dowell), 81
Thompson
 Catharine, 68

Raleigh, 68
Sally, 68
William, 103
Thornburgh
Hannah, 58
Thurman
Cordelia, 111
George B., 77
Lucy Ann, 77
Timms
Elisha, 52
Toler
Tabitha T. (Carroll), 41
William B., 41
Tool
Richard, 2
Sarah, 2
Toone
Argelon, 19
Topping
Malinda S., 101
tracts
Blackwater, 48
Blandford, 12
Hatcher's run plantation, 48
Horse Pasture, 7
Marrow Bone, 7
Poison Field, 7
Saints Hill, 28
Shirley, 28
Skipwith, 48
Traylor
Mr., 48
Treasurers, 3, 5, 6
trials, 1
troops, 25
Trueman
John, 51
Rebecca, 51
Tucker
James, 17
John, 62
Tuggle
Henry, 79
tuition
poor children, 72
Tunis
Douglass, 65
Maria (Howard), 65
Turnell
Richard, 109
Rosa, 109
Turner
Kinchen, 111
Nancy, 13
Sarah (Pierce), 111

Thomas, 28
Thomizen Elzey, 52
William, 16
Turpin
Edwin, 48
Tyler Co., Va., 76, 90

U
U.S. Army, 4, 21, 64
U.S. Marines, 16
unchaste conduct, 13
unsound mind, 65
Upshur
George Littleton, 74
John Henry, 74

V
Vance
Daniel H., 58
Elias, 58
William Buse, 58
Vanmeter
Abraham, 60, 61
Elizabeth, 60, 61
Vansant
James, 113
Mary, 113
Verser
Daniel, 55
vessels, 40
Virginia Journal and
Alexandria Advertiser, 107
Vizzoneau
Andre Thomas, 72
Mary Anne, 72

W
Wade
Sally, 70
Wagener
Margaret S., 50
Margaret S. (Harrison), 50
Waldo
John Jones, 52
Walker
James, 23
John S., 34
William, 34
Walkley
Mary, 51
Warden
Malachi, 78

Margaret Ann, 78
Wardsworth
Jane L., 70
Warner
Oney (Jourdan), 23
Osborn, 23
warrants, 9, 14, 15, 19, 24, 25, 29, 32, 34, 38, 43, 44, 51, 54, 62, 71, 75, 79, 93, 105
Warrell
Thomas, 29
wars, 2, 4-6, 19
1812, 93
Revolutionary, 16, 21, 31, 38, 39, 43, 44, 51, 54, 58, 62, 104
with Mexico, 93, 105
Warwick
Ann Eliza (Ross), 110
Henry D., 110
Sally B., 16
Washington
George, Gen., 21
George, will of, 105
John, 28
John Love, 28
Washington Co., Va., 28
Washington, D.C., 113
Waterman
Sarah, 55
Watkins
Edward, 48
Henry E., 48
Watson
Elizabeth, 71
Richard P., 71
Watt
George, 15
Watts
James L., 64
Lucy, 64
Wayne Co., Va., 91, 103
Webb
Benajah A., 111
Frances, 111
Weddell
Mary Anne, 69
Weeden
William, 52
Wells
John James, 98
Welman
John, 103
West
Alexander, 58
John, 58

Thomas, 10
West Indies, 31, 40
West Point, 6
Westmoreland Co., Va., 44
Wharton
  Barney, 60
  Lemuel, 60
  Lewis, 60
  Nancy, 60
  William, 60
White
  Elizabeth B., 110
  George, 52
  Grafton, 17
  Henrietta, 11
  John L., 110
Whitlock
  Patty, 46
Wilkinson
  J.B., 22
Williams
  Delilah, 107
  John W., 92
  Mildred C. (Tate), 59
  Richard, 48
  Sarah D., 92
  William B., 59
Williamsburg, Va., 22, 58
  hospital at, 53
Willis
  George, 5
Wilson
  Indiana, 69
  John, 46, 69, 102
  Josiah, 69
  Mary E., 69
  Patty (Whitlock), 46
  Sarah F., 102
Winchester, Va.
  Chancery Court, 36
Wingfield
  Mary E.S., 101
Wingoe
  Susanna, 11
Winsor
  John A., 52
Wirt
  William, 12
Wishart
  William, 14
Withers
  Catharine, 82
woman of colour, 16, 37, 63,
  76, 109
Wood
  Henry, 56

Wood Co., Va., 22
  sundry citizens of, 52
wood lands, 60
woods, 48
Woodyard
  Amanda (Johnson), 84
  John, 84
Woolfolk
  Anna (Roane), 103
  Bentley B., 103
Wright
  Benjamin, 78
  Mariam, 78
  Paulina (Pendleton), 84
  Shelton, 84
writs, 14
Wyoming Co., Va., 101
Wythe Co., Va., 53

Y

Yancey
  Charles, 23
Yeaman
  John, 55
Yeaton
  William, 105
Yonson
  Eliza Jane, 90
  William, 90
York Co., Va., 24, 63
York, Siege of, 38

No Surname
[ ]
  Aggy, 37
  Anne, 20
  Betty, 20
  Billy, 22
  Celia, 20
  Charles, 18
  Cynthia, 18
  Elizabeth, 16
  Fanny, 22
  Frank, 16
  Hannah, 22
  Harry, 20
  Henry, 16, 20
  John, 22
  Lavington, 40
  Lissey, 20
  Margaret, 63
  Maria, 29
  Mary, 22
  Milly, 20
  Molly, 22
  Nelson, 40
  Patience, 16
  Pheda, 20
  Philemon, 16
  Philip, 40
  Polly, 20
  Priscilla, 20, 22
  Sarah, 20, 22
  Spencer, 20
  Stephen, 19
  Susan, 22
  Walter, 20
  Washington, 22
  William, 29
  Zack, 22

Other Books by Wesley E. Pippenger:

Alexandria (Arlington) County, Virginia Death Records, 1853-1896

Alexandria City and Arlington County, Virginia Records Index: Vol. 1

Alexandria City and Arlington County, Virginia Records Index: Vol. 2

Alexandria County, Virginia Marriage Records, 1853-1895

Alexandria Virginia Marriage Index, January 10, 1893 to August 31, 1905

Alexandria, Virginia Marriages, 1870-1892

Alexandria, Virginia Town Lots, 1749-1801
Together with the Proceedings of the Board of Trustees, 1749-1780

Alexandria, Virginia Wills, Administrations and Guardianships, 1786-1800

Alexandria, Virginia 1808 Census (Wards 1, 2, 3, and 4)

Alexandria, Virginia Death Records, 1863-1896

Alexandria, Virginia Hustings Court Orders, Volume 1, 1780-1787

Connections and Separations: Divorce, Name Change and Other
Genealogical Tidbits from the Acts of the Virginia General Assembly

Daily National Intelligencer *Index to Deaths, 1855-1870*

Daily National Intelligencer, *Washington, District of Columbia*
Marriages and Deaths Notices (January 1, 1851 to December 30, 1854)

Dead People on the Move: Reconstruction of the Georgetown Presbyterian Burying Ground,
Holmead's (Western) Burying Ground, and other Removals in the District of Columbia

Death Notices from Richmond, Virginia Newspapers, 1841-1853

District of Columbia Ancestors, A Guide to Records of the District of Columbia

District of Columbia Death Records: August 1, 1874-July 31, 1879

District of Columbia Foreign Deaths, 1888-1923

District of Columbia Guardianship Index, 1802-1928

District of Columbia Interments (Index to Deaths)
January 1, 1855 to July 31, 1874

District of Columbia Marriage Licenses, Register 1: 1811-1858

District of Columbia Marriage Licenses, Register 2: 1858-1870

District of Columbia Marriage Records Index, 1877-1885

District of Columbia Marriage Records Index
October 20, 1885 to January 20, 1892: Marriage Record Books 21 to 30

District of Columbia Probate Records, 1801-1852

District of Columbia: Original Land Owners, 1791-1800

Early Church Records of Alexandria City and Fairfax County, Virginia

Georgetown, District of Columbia 1850 Federal Population Census (Schedule I)
and 1853 Directory of Residents of Georgetown

Georgetown, District of Columbia Marriage and Death Notices, 1801-1838

Husbands and Wives Associated with Early Alexandria, Virginia
(and the Surrounding Area), 3rd Edition, Revised

Index to Virginia Estates, 1800-1865
Volumes 4, 5 and 6

John Alexander, a Northern Neck Proprietor, His Family, Friends and Kin

Legislative Petitions of Alexandria, 1778-1861

Pippenger and Pittenger Families

Proceedings of the Orphan's Court, Washington County, District of Columbia, 1801-1808

The Georgetown Courier *Marriage and Death Notices: Georgetown, District of Columbia, November 18, 1865 to May 6, 1876*

The Georgetown Directory for the Year 1830: to which is appended, a Short Description of the Churches, Public Institutions, and the Original Charter of Georgetown, and Extracts of the Laws Pertaining to the Chesapeake and Ohio Canal Company

The Virginia Gazette and Alexandria Advertiser:
Volume 1, September 3, 1789 to November 11, 1790

The Virginia Journal and Alexandria Advertiser:
Volume I (February 5, 1784 to January 27, 1785)

Volume II (February 3, 1785 to January 26, 1786)

Volume III (March 2, 1786 to January 25, 1787)

Volume IV (February 8, 1787 to May 21, 1789)

The Washington and Georgetown Directory of 1853

Tombstone Inscriptions of Alexandria, Volumes 1-4

www.ingramcontent.com/pod-product-compliance
Lightning Source LLC
Chambersburg PA
CBHW071813090426
42737CB00012B/2072